D0881112

Interpretation and Social Criticism

The Tanner Lectures on Human Values   1985

INTERPRETATION
— AND —
SOCIAL CRITICISM

Michael Walzer

HARVARD UNIVERSITY PRESS
Cambridge, Massachusetts, and London, England   1987

Library of Congress Cataloging-in-Publication Data

Walzer, Michael.
    Interpretation and social criticism.

    (The Tanner lectures)
    Includes index.
    1. Hermeneutics.   2. Ethics.   3. Social sciences—
Philosophy.   I. Title.   II. Series.
BD241.W345   1987   300'.1   86-14997
ISBN 0-674-45970-9 (alk. paper)

Designed by Gwen Frankfeldt

For J.B.W.

PREFACE

My aim in this book is to provide a philosophical framework for the understanding of social criticism as a social
practice. What do social critics do? How do they go about
doing it? Where do their principles come from? How do
critics establish their distance from the people and institutions they criticize? The argument sustained throughout
the book, that social criticism is best understood as critical
interpretation, runs parallel to arguments made in recent
years by European philosophers. But I have tried to find
my own way, in my own language, without direct reference to their work. I hope to publish in the near future a
larger book dealing with the practice of criticism in the
twentieth century—a more explicitly political book, for
which this book constitutes a theoretical preamble. There I
will have occasion to address the question, as much political as it is philosophical, whether social criticism is possible without "critical theory."

The first two chapters were given as the Tanner Lectures on Human Values at Harvard University on Novem-
ber 13 and 14, 1985, and are published here by permission
of the Trustees of the Tanner Lectures on Human Values.
The third chapter was read to Harvard Hillel on Novem-
ber 15. The three were written at roughly the same time,
employ the same vocabulary, and make the same arguments; they belong together, the last supplying what the

first two largely lack: some degree of historical concreteness and specificity.

I am grateful to the many members of the Harvard community, critics all, who attended the lectures and explained to me where I had gone wrong. My revisions certainly reflect their criticism—especially that of Martha Minow, Michael Sandel, Thomas Scanlon, Judith Shklar, and Lloyd Weinreb—though the reflection is probably, as often as not, obscure and incomplete. "The Prophet as Social Critic," in an earlier version, was discussed at a symposium on prophecy at Drew University and published in the *Drew Gateway* along with a helpful response by Henry French. A number of people at the Institute for Advanced Study read the lectures for me and commented on them in detail: Clifford Geertz, Don Herzog, Michael Rustin, and Alan Wertheimer. They had a lot to do with, though they are not responsible for, their final form.

CONTENTS

Interpretation and Social Criticism

Three Paths in Moral Philosophy

D ESPITE the title of this chapter, I shall not argue that there are three and only three ways of doing moral philosophy. My purpose is not to suggest an exhaustive list, only to look at three common and important approaches to the subject. I call these the path of discovery, the path of invention, and the path of interpretation. I mean to describe the last as the one (of the three) that accords best with our everyday experience of morality. Then in the next chapter I shall try to defend interpretation against the charge that it binds us irrevocably to the status quo—since we can only interpret what already exists— and so undercuts the very possibility of social criticism. Since criticism is a feature of everyday morality, the charge has a twofold character: it suggests not only that interpretation is a bad program for, but also that it is a bad account of, moral experience. It is, as they say, neither normatively nor descriptively correct. I shall argue against both these aspects of the charge—proceeding in this chapter by way of theoretical contrast, in the next one by way of practical example; focusing more on the account here, more on the program there—but not tying myself to this simple and probably misleading division. The last chapter will bring account and program together in an extended historical analysis of social criticism, specifically of biblical prophecy, in the interpretive mode.

WE KNOW the path of discovery first and best from the history of religion. Here, to be sure, discovery waits upon revelation; but someone must climb the mountain, go into the desert, seek out the God-who-reveals, and bring back his word. This person is for the rest of us the discoverer of the moral law: if God reveals it to him, he reveals it to us. Like the physical world, like life itself, morality is a creation; but we are not its creators. God makes it, and we come, with his help and with the help of his servants, to know about it and then to admire and study it. Religious morality commonly takes the form of a written text, a sacred book, and so it requires interpretation. But we first experience it through the medium of discovery. The moral world is like a new continent, and the religious leader (God's servant) is like an explorer who brings us the good news of its existence and the first map of its shape.

I should note one significant feature of this map. The moral world is not only divinely created; it is constituted by divine commands. What is revealed to us is a set of decrees: do this! don't do that! And these decrees are critical in character, critical from the beginning, for it would hardly be a revelation if God commanded us to do and not do what we were already doing and not doing. A revealed morality will always stand in sharp contrast to old ideas and practices. That may well be its chief advantage. But it is, necessarily, a short-lived advantage, for once the revelation is accepted, once the new moral world is inhabited, the critical edge is lost. Now God's decrees—so at least we pretend to ourselves—regulate our everyday behavior; we are what he wants us to be. Any morality that has once been discovered, of course, can always be rediscovered. The claim to have found again some long-lost or corrupted doctrine is the basis of every religious and moral reformation. But God is not present now in the same way as he was in the beginning. Rediscovery does not wait upon revelation; it is our own work, archaeological in form; and we have to interpret what we dig up. The moral law rediscovered lacks the blazing clarity of its first coming.

I mean this brief account of religious morality as a prelude to a more secular story. There are natural as well as divine revelations, and a philosopher who reports to us on the existence of natural law, say, or natural rights or any set of objective moral truths has walked the path of discovery. Perhaps he has walked it as a kind of moral anthropologist, searching for what is natural in what is real. More likely, given the standard form of the philosophical enterprise, the search is internal, mental, a matter of detachment and reflection. The moral world comes into view as the philosopher steps back in his mind from his social position. He wrenches himself loose from his parochial interests and loyalties; he abandons his own point of view and looks at the world, as Thomas Nagel argues, from "no particular point of view." [1] The project is at least as heroic as climbing the mountain or marching into the desert. "No particular point of view" is somewhere on the way to God's point of view, and what the philosopher sees from there is something like objective value. That is, if I understand the argument, he sees himself and all the others, himself no different from the others, and he recognizes the moral principles that necessarily govern the relations of creatures like those.

1. Nagel, "The Limits of Objectivity," in *The Tanner Lectures on Human Values,* vol. I (Salt Lake City: Utah University Press, 1980), p. 83. Cf. Nagel, *The View from Nowhere* (Oxford: Oxford University Press, 1986).

The necessity, clearly, is moral, not practical, else we would not have to step back to discover it. Hence the principles, once again, are critical principles; they exist at some distance from our parochial practices and opinions. And once we have discovered them, or once they have been announced to us, we ought to incorporate them into our everyday moral life. But I confess to less confidence in this secular discovery than in the earlier religious discovery. Most often, the moral principles here delivered to us are already in our possession, incorporated, as it were, long ago, familiar and well-thumbed by now. Philosophical discovery is likely to fall short of the radical newness and sharp specificity of divine revelation. Accounts of natural law or natural rights rarely ring true as descriptions of a new moral world. Consider Nagel's discovery of an objective moral principle: that we should not be indifferent to the suffering of other people.[2] I acknowledge the principle but miss the excitement of revelation. I knew that already. What is involved in discoveries of this sort is something like a dis-incorporation of moral principles, so that we can see them, not for the first time but freshly, stripped of encrusted interests and prejudices. Seen in this way, the principles may well look objective; we "know" them in much the same way as religious men and women know the divine law. They are, so to speak, *there,* waiting to be enforced. But they are only there because they are really here, features of ordinary life.

I do not mean to deny the reality of the experience of stepping back, though I doubt that we can ever step back

2. "Limits of Objectivity," pp. 109–110. Nagel's own social criticism relies on more substantive principles, but I am not sure to what extent these are "objective" principles. See Nagel, *Mortal Questions* (Cambridge: Cambridge University Press, 1979), chs. 5–8.

all the way to nowhere. Even when we look at the world from *somewhere else,* however, we are still looking at the world. We are looking, in fact, at a particular world; we may see it with special clarity, but we will not discover anything that isn't already there. Since the particular world is also our own world, we will not discover anything that isn't already here. Perhaps this is a general truth about secular (moral) discoveries; if so, it suggests what we lose when we lose our belief in God.

But I have been assuming a philosopher who strains to see more clearly, if only in abstract outline, the moral reality in front of him. One can, by contrast, call that reality into question and set out in search of a deeper truth, like a physicist piercing the atom. The moral philosophy called utilitarianism, based on the deepest truth about human desire and aversion, was probably discovered in this way. Godless in its origins and radically unfamiliar in its outcomes, utilitarianism suggests what we gain by the imitation of science. Bentham obviously believed that he had come upon a set of objective principles, and the applications of these principles are, very often, not recognizable at all as features of ordinary life.[3] Frightened by the strangeness of their own arguments, most utilitarian philosophers fiddle with the felicific calculus so that it yields results closer to what we all think. So they pull the exception back to the rule: without confidence in revelation, we can only

3. Bentham suggests that utilitarianism is the only plausible account of what ordinary people think about morality, but his ambition goes far beyond providing such an account. He claims to have discovered the foundation of morality: "Nature has placed mankind under the governance of two sovereign masters, pain and pleasure. It is for them alone to point out what we ought to do." *The Principles of Morals and Legislation,* ch. 1. The rest of the *Principles* suggests that these two masters do not always point to what ordinary people think *they* ought to do.

discover what we know. Philosophy is a second coming (lower case), which brings us not millennial understanding but the wisdom of the owl at dusk. There is, though, this alternative, which I find more frightening than attractive: the wisdom of the eagle at daybreak.

MANY PEOPLE, perhaps for good reasons, will not be satisfied with the wisdom of the owl. Some will deny its objectivity, despite the detachment of the philosophers who seek it out; but that is not a denial I want to defend. I am inclined to agree with Nagel's sardonic view of the skeptic's questions: What reason can I possibly have for *not* being indifferent to my neighbor's pain? What reason can I have for caring, even a little bit? Nagel writes: "As an expression of puzzlement, [this] has that characteristic philosophical craziness which indicates that something very fundamental has gone wrong."[4] Yes, but what is more worrisome than this craziness is the sense I have already expressed, that the moral principles revealed in this or that undoubtedly sane philosophy lack the special edge, the critical force, of divine revelation. "Don't be indifferent" is not at all the same thing as "Love thy neighbor as thyself." And the second of these is unlikely to figure in the list of philosophical discoveries—if only because the question, Why should I love him *that much?* is not crazy. The principle of nonindifference, or more positively, the principle of minimal concern, is conceivably a critical principle, but its strength is uncertain. A great deal of work would have to be done—and it is not clear that it could be done by a man or woman standing nowhere in particular,

4. "Limits of Objectivity," p. 110.

or even by a man or woman standing somewhere else—to work out its relation to everyday social practice.

On the other hand, men and women standing nowhere in particular could construct an entirely new moral world—imitating God's creation rather than the discoveries of his servants. They might undertake to do this because they thought that there was no actually existing moral world (because God was dead, or mankind radically alienated from nature, or nature devoid of moral meaning); or they might undertake the construction because they thought that the actually existing moral world was inadequate or that our knowledge of it could never be, as knowledge, sufficiently critical in character. We might think of this undertaking in terms Descartes suggests when he describes his intellectual project: "to reform my own thoughts and to build on a foundation wholly my own." In fact, I suppose, Descartes was really launched on a journey of discovery, "like a man who walks alone, and in the dark," searching for objective truth.[5] But in the analogies that leap to his mind, there is no objective truth to discover, and the project is explicitly constructive in character:

So I thought to myself that the peoples who were formerly half savages, and who became civilized only gradually, making their laws only insofar as the harm done by crimes and quarrels forced them to do so, could not be so well organized as those who, from the moment at which they came together in association, observed the basic laws of some wise legislator; just as it is indeed certain that the state of the true religion, the laws of which God alone has made, must be incomparably better or-

5. Descartes, *Discourse on Method*, trans. F. E. Sutcliffe (Harmondsworth: Penguin, 1968), pp. 38, 39.

dered than all the others. And, to speak of human things, I believe that, if Sparta greatly flourished in times past, it was not on account of the excellence of each of its laws taken individually, seeing that many were very strange and even contrary to good morals, but because, having been invented by one man only, they all tended towards the same end.[6]

This is the path of invention; the end is given by the morality we hope to invent. The end is a common life, where justice, or political virtue, or goodness, or some such basic value would be realized.

So we are to design the moral world under this condition: that there is no pre-existent design, no divine or natural blueprint to guide us. How should we proceed? We need a discourse on method for moral philosophy, and most philosophers who have walked the path of invention have begun with methodology: a design of a design procedure. (The existentialists, who do not begin that way, though they are clearly commited to an invented morality, are of little help in the business of invention.) The crucial requirement of a design procedure is that it eventuate in agreement. Hence the work of Descartes's legislator is very risky unless he is a representative figure, somehow embodying the range of opinions and interests that are in play around him. We cannot adopt the simple expedient of making the legislator omnipotent, a rational and benevolent despot, for that would be to settle a basic feature of the design—the just distribution of power—before the design procedure had even gotten started. The legislator must somehow be authorized to speak for all of us, or alternatively, all of us must be present and accounted for from the beginning. It is not easy to see how we might choose a

6. *Discourse on Method,* p. 36.

representative, a proxy for humankind. But if we give up on representation and opt for the alternative, universal presence, we are more likely to produce cacophony than order, and the outcome will be "more the product of chance," as Descartes writes, "than . . . of a human will operating according to reason."[7]

There are a variety of solutions to this problem; the best known and most elegant is that of John Rawls.[8] The Rawlsian solution has the nice result that it ceases to matter whether the constructive or legislative work is undertaken by a single person or by many people. Deprived of all knowledge of their standing in the social world, of their interests, values, talents, and relationships, potential legislators are rendered, for the practical purposes at hand, identical. It makes no difference whether such people talk to one another or one among them talks only to himself: one person talking is enough. Other proposed solutions (that of Jürgen Habermas, for example) are more cumbersome, requiring that we imagine actual conversations, but only in circumstances carefully designed to lift the discourse above the level of ideological confrontation.[9] The partici-

7. *Discourse on Method*, p. 35.

8. Rawls, *A Theory of Justice* (Cambridge, Massachusetts: Harvard University Press, 1971).

9. Habermas, *Communication and the Evolution of Society*, trans. Thomas McCarthy (Boston: Beacon, 1979), esp. ch. 1. But there is a dilemma here: if the circumstances of what Habermas calls ideal speech or undistorted communication are specified in detail, then only a limited number of things can be said, and these things could probably be said by the philosopher himself, representing all the rest of us. It is not as if we have a real choice about what opinions we will finally form. See Raymond Geuss, *The Idea of a Critical Theory: Habermas and the Frankfurt School* (Cambridge: Cambridge University Press, 1981), p. 72. If, however, the circumstances are only roughly specified, so that ideal speech resembles a democratic debate, then the participants can say almost anything, and there is no reason why the results should not (sometimes) turn out to be "very strange and even contrary to good morals."

pants must be liberated from the bonds of particularism, else they will never produce the rational outcome that they require, namely, a moral world so designed that all of them are prepared to live in it, and to think it just, whatever place they come to occupy, whatever projects they come to pursue.

Assume the death of God or the meaninglessness of nature—apparently painless assumptions in these latter days—and then we can say of these legislators that they invent the moral world that would have existed if a moral world had existed without their inventing it. They create what God would have created if there were a God. This is not the only way of describing what happens on the path of invention. Descartes's Spartan analogy suggests a different view, which I think is also Rawls's view, a minimalist version of inventiveness. What Lycurgus creates is not the best city, the city that God would have created, but only the best city for the Spartans, the work, as it were, of a Spartan god. I will want to come back to this possibility later on. I need to consider first the stronger claim that the moral world we invent behind the veil of ignorance or through an ideologically uncluttered conversation is the only world we could invent, universally inhabitable, a world for all persons.

The critical force of an invented morality is more like that of divine law than philosophical discovery (or, it is closer to the wisdom of the eagle than the owl). Rawls's difference principle, to take a much discussed example, has something of the novelty and specificity of revelation. No one would think of saying that it was just plain crazy to call it into question. As divine law derives its force from its creator, so the difference principle derives its force from the process by which it was created. If we accept it, it is because we have participated, or can imagine ourselves having participated, in its invention. And if we invent one such principle, we can obviously invent others as we need them; or we can deduce from the one a whole system of rules and regulations. Bruce Ackerman, in his discussion of liberal justice, manages to cover a range of issues roughly equivalent to that covered by the Exodus and Deuteronomic codes—though his revelation is delivered not to one but to every actual and imaginable nation.[10] So we create a morality against which we can measure any person's life, any society's practices.

It is not the case, of course, that the lives and practices we measure are morally meaningless until we measure them. They embody their own values, which are distorted—so philosophers of invention must believe—by a radically imperfect design procedure. These values are created by conversation, argument, and political negotiation in circumstances we might best call social, over long periods of time. The point of an invented morality is to provide what God and nature do not provide, a universal corrective for all the different social moralities. But why should we bow to universal correction? What exactly is the critical force of the philosopher's invention—assuming, still, that it is the only possible invention? I will try to answer these questions by telling a story of my own, a story meant to parallel and heighten certain features of the Rawlsian account of what happens in the original position: a caricature, I am afraid, for which I apologize in advance; but caricature has its uses.[11]

---

10. Ackerman, *Social Justice in the Liberal State* (New Haven: Yale University Press, 1980).

11. The caricature is aimed at Rawls's epigones rather than at Rawls himself, who would probably not accept its first stipulation.

Imagine, then, that a group of travelers from different countries and different moral cultures, speaking different languages, meet in some neutral space (like outer space). They have to cooperate, at least temporarily, and if they are to cooperate, each of them must refrain from insisting upon his or her own values and practices. Hence we deny them knowledge of their own values and practices; and since that knowledge is not only personal but also social, embodied in language itself, we obliterate their linguistic memories and require them to think and talk (temporarily) in some pidgin language that is equally parasitic on all their natural languages—a more perfect Esperanto. What principles of cooperation would they adopt? I shall assume that there is a single answer to this question and that the principles given in that answer properly govern their life together in the space they now occupy. That seems plausible enough; the design procedure is genuinely useful for the purposes at hand. What is less plausible is that the travelers should be required to carry those same principles with them when they go home. Why should newly invented principles govern the lives of people who already share a moral culture and speak a natural language?

Men and women standing behind the veil of ignorance, deprived of all knowledge of their own way of life, forced to live with other men and women similarly deprived, will perhaps, with whatever difficulties, find a *modus vivendi*—not a way of life but a way of living. But even if this is the only possible *modus vivendi* for these people in these conditions, it does not follow that it is a universally valuable arrangement. (It might, of course, have a kind of heuristic value—many things have heuristic value—but I will not pursue that possibility now.) There seems to be a confusion here: it is as if we were to take a hotel room or an accommodation apartment or a safe house as the ideal model of a human home. Away from home, we are grateful for the shelter and convenience of a hotel room. Deprived of all knowledge of what our own home was like, talking with people similarly deprived, required to design rooms that any one of us might live in, we would probably come up with something like, but not quite so culturally specific as, the Hilton Hotel. With this difference: we would not allow luxury suites; all the rooms would be exactly the same; or if there were luxury suites, their only purpose would be to bring more business to the hotel and enable us to improve all the other rooms, starting with those most in need of improvement. But even if the improvements went pretty far, we might still long for the homes we knew we once had but could no longer remember. We would not be morally bound to live in the hotel we had designed.

I have been assuming that my own view of hotels is widely shared, and so I should note one telling dissent—a line from Franz Kafka's journal: "I like hotel rooms. I always feel immediately at home in hotel rooms, more than at home, really." [12] Note the irony: there is no other way to convey the sense of being in one's own place except to say "at home." It is a hard thing to suggest to men and women that they give up the moral comfort that those words evoke. But what if they do not share that comfort? What if their lives are like that of Kafka's K., or of any twentieth-century exile, outcast, refugee, or stateless person? For such people, hotels are very important. They need the protection of the rooms, decent (if bare) human

12. Quoted in Ernst Pawel, *The Nightmare of Reason: A Life of Franz Kafka* (New York: Farrar, Straus, and Giroux, 1984), p. 191.

accommodation. They need a universal (if minimal) morality, or at least a morality worked out among strangers. What they commonly *want,* however, is not to be permanently registered in a hotel but to be established in a new home, a dense moral culture within which they can feel some sense of belonging.

Thus far my story. But there is another, more plausible way of thinking about the process of moral invention. Let us assume that the actually existing (social) moralities incorporate, as they claim to do, divine commands or natural laws or, at least, genuinely valuable moral principles however these are understood. Our purpose now is not invention *de novo;* rather, we need to construct an account or a model of some existing morality that gives us a clear and comprehensive view of the critical force of its own principles, without the intervening confusion of prejudice or self-interest. Hence we do not meet with travelers in outer space but with fellow members in inner or social space. We consult our own moral understandings, our reflective awareness of principle, but we try to filter out, even to bar entirely, any sense of personal ambition or advantage. Our method, once again, is epistemic denial, which functions now, according to Rawls, as a "device of representation."[13] So we surrender all knowledge of our position in society and of our private connections and commitments, but not, this time, of the values (like liberty and equality) that we share. We want to describe the moral world in which we live from "no particular point of view" within that world. Though the description is carefully designed and its immediate conditions are highly artificial, it

13. Rawls, "Justice as Fairness: Political Not Metaphysical," *Philosophy and Public Affairs* 14.3 (1985): 236.

is nonetheless a description of something real. Hence it is more like philosophical discovery than divine revelation. The inventiveness of the philosopher consists only in turning moral reality into an ideal type.

The idealized morality is in origin a social morality; it is neither divine nor natural, except insofar as we believe that "the voice of the people is the voice of God" or that human nature requires us to live in society—and neither of these views commits us to approve of everything the people say or of every social arrangement. The project of modeling or idealizing an existing morality does depend, however, upon some prior acknowledgment of the value of that morality. Perhaps its value is simply this: that there is no other starting point for moral speculation. We have to start from where we are. Where we are, however, is always *someplace of value,* else we would never have settled there. Some such argument, it seems to me, is equally as important for invention in its second, minimalist version as for interpretation. Its importance is conceded by philosophers of invention who appeal to our intuitions, sometimes in constructing, sometimes in testing, their models and ideal types. Intuition is a prereflective, prephilosophic knowledge of the moral world; it resembles the account a blind man might give of the furnishings of a familiar house. The familiarity is crucial. Moral philosophy is here understood as a reflection upon the familiar, a reinvention of our own homes.

This is, however, a critical reflection, reinvention with a purpose: we are to correct our intuitions by reference to the model we construct out of those same intuitions, or we are to correct our more groping intuitions by reference to a model we construct out of our more confident intuitions. We move back and forth in either case between moral immediacy and moral abstraction, between an intuitive and a reflective understanding.[14] But what is it that we are trying to understand? And how does our understanding of it, whatever it is, acquire critical force? Clearly, at this point, we are not trying to understand divine law or to grasp an objective morality; nor are we trying to build an entirely new city. Our focus is on ourselves, our own principles and values—otherwise, intuition would be no help. Since this is also the focus of those committed to the path of interpretation, I want to turn to them. They also face in an especially direct way the problem of critical force. Given that every interpretation is parasitic on its "text," how can it ever constitute an adequate criticism of the text?

THE ARGUMENT thus far is usefully summarized by way of an analogy. The three paths in moral philosophy can be compared, roughly, to the three branches of government. Discovery resembles the work of the executive: to find, proclaim, and then enforce the law. Enforcement is not, I admit, a common philosophical task, but those who believe that they have discovered the true moral law are likely enough to want or, whatever their private preferences, to believe themselves duty bound to enforce it. Moses exemplifies this reluctant sense of duty. Irreligious writers like Machiavelli have called him a legislator, but if we attend to the biblical account, we see that he did not legislate at all; he received the law, taught it to the people, and strove to see that it was obeyed; he was an unwilling

14. See Norman Daniels, "Wide Reflective Equilibrium and Theory Acceptance in Ethics," *Journal of Philosophy* 76.5 (1979): 256–282.

but at least occasionally energetic political leader. The obvious philosophical parallel is Plato's philosopher-king, who does not create the good, but finds it, and then sets himself, with similar reluctance, to enact it in the world. Utilitarianism provides more straightforward examples, as does Marxism, another example of scientific discovery.

Discovery is not itself execution; it simply points toward executive authority. But invention is legislative from the beginning, for philosophical inventors mean to invest their principles with the force of (moral) law. That is why invention is the work of representative men and women, who stand for us all because they could be any one of us. But invention is of two sorts, and these two correspond to two different sorts of lawmaking and require two different sorts of representation. Invention *de novo* is like constitutional legislation. The lawmakers, since they are creating a new moral world, must represent every possible or potential member, that is, everybody, wherever he lives and whatever his current values and commitments. Minimalist invention is more like the work of legal codification. Now the lawmakers, since what they are codifying already exists, must represent the people for whom it exists, that is, a group of men and women who share intuitions, who are committed to a particular set of principles, however confused that set may be.

Codification is obviously an interpretive as well as an inventive or constructive enterprise: here the second path runs close to the third. Still, a code is a law or a system of laws, while an interpretation is a judgment, the proper work of the judicial branch. The claim of interpretation is simply this: that neither discovery nor invention is necessary because we already possess what they pretend to provide. Morality, unlike politics, does not require executive authority or systematic legislation. We do not have to discover the moral world because we have always lived there. We do not have to invent it because it has already been invented—though not in accordance with any philosophical method. No design procedure has governed its design, and the result no doubt is disorganized and uncertain. It is also very dense: the moral world has a lived-in quality, like a home occupied by a single family over many generations, with unplanned additions here and there, and all the available space filled with memory-laden objects and artifacts. The whole thing, taken as a whole, lends itself less to abstract modeling than to thick description. Moral argument in such a setting is interpretive in character, closely resembling the work of a lawyer or judge who struggles to find meaning in a morass of conflicting laws and precedents.

But lawyers and judges, it might be said, are bound to the legal morass; it is their business to find meaning there, and they have no business looking elsewhere. The legal morass, or better, the meaning that can be found within it, is authoritative for them. But why should the moral morass be authoritative for philosophers? Why shouldn't they look elsewhere, in search of a better authority? The morality we discover is authoritative because God made it or because it is objectively true. The morality we invent is authoritative because anyone would invent it, could only invent it, so long as he adopted the proper design procedure and worked at the proper distance from his immediate, parochial self. But why is this existing morality authoritative—this morality that just *is,* the product of time, accident, external force, political compromise, fallible and particularist intentions? The easiest way to answer this question would be to insist that the moralities we discover and invent always turn out, and always will turn out, remarkably similar to the morality we already have. Philosophical discovery and invention (leaving aside divine revelation) are disguised interpretations; there is really only one path in moral philosophy. I am tempted by this view, even though it does not do justice to the sincere ambition or, sometimes, the dangerous presumption of discoverers and inventors. But I do not want to deny that it is possible to walk the first two paths, nor to assert that people doing that are really doing something else. There are indeed discoveries and inventions—utilitarianism is one example—but the more novel these are, the less likely they are to make for strong or even plausible arguments. The experience of moral argument is best understood in the interpretive mode. What we do when we argue is to give an account of the actually existing morality. That morality is authoritative for us because it is only by virtue of its existence that we exist as the moral beings we are. Our categories, relationships, commitments, and aspirations are all shaped by, expressed in terms of, the existing morality. Discovery and invention are efforts at escape, in the hope of finding some external and universal standard with which to judge moral existence. The effort may well be commendable, but it is, I think, unnecessary. The critique of existence begins, or can begin, from principles internal to existence itself.

One might say that the moral world is authoritative for us because it provides us with everything we need to live a moral life, including the capacity for reflection and criticism. No doubt some moralities are more "critical" than others, but that does not mean they are better (or worse). It is more likely that they provide, roughly, what their protagonists need. At the same time, the capacity for criticism always extends beyond the "needs" of the social structure itself and its dominant groups. I do not want to defend a functionalist position. The moral world and the social world are more or less coherent, but they are never more than more or less coherent. Morality is always potentially subversive of class and power.

I will try in Chapter 2 to say why subversion is always possible and how it actually works. But I need now to elaborate on the claim that moral argument is most often interpretive in character. The claim seems more plausible with regard to the judicial analogy. For the question commonly posed to lawyers and judges takes a form that invites interpretation: what is the legal or the constitutional thing to do? The reference of the question is to a particular body of laws or to a particular constitutional text, and there is no way to answer the question except by giving an account of the laws or the text. Neither the one nor the other has the simplicity and precision of a yardstick against which we might measure the different actions urged by the contending parties. Deprived of a yardstick, we rely on exegesis, commentary, and historical precedent, a tradition of argument and interpretation. Any given interpretation will be contentious, of course, but there is little disagreement about what it is that we are interpreting or about the need for the interpretive effort.

But the question commonly posed to ordinary men and women arguing about morality has a different form: what is the right thing to do? And now it is not clear at all what the reference of the question is or how we are to go about answering it. It does not appear that the question is about the interpretation of an existing and particular morality, for it is possible that that morality, however interpreted, does not tell us the right thing to do. Perhaps we should search for, or invent, a better morality. But if we follow the course of the argument, listen to it, study its phenomenology, we will see that its real subject is the meaning of the particular moral life shared by the protagonists. The general question about the right thing to do is quickly turned into some more specific question—about the career open to talents, let's say, and then about equal opportunity, affirmative action, and quotas. These can be read as matters of constitutional law, requiring legal interpretation; but they are also moral matters. And they then require us to argue about what a career is, what sorts of talents we ought to recognize, whether equal opportunity is a "right," and if it is, what social policies it mandates. These questions are pursued within a tradition of moral discourse—indeed, they only arise within that tradition— and they are pursued by interpreting the terms of that discourse.[15] The argument is about ourselves; the meaning of our way of life is what is at issue. The general question we finally answer is not quite the one we asked at first. It has a crucial addition: what is the right thing *for us* to do?

It is nonetheless true that the moral question is commonly put in more general terms than the legal question. The reason for this can only be that morality is in fact more general than law. Morality provides those basic pro-

---

15. In a society where children inherited the employments and positions of their parents and learned what they needed to know about those employments and positions largely from their parents, the "career open to talents" would not be a plausible or perhaps even a comprehensible idea. Planning a career is not a universal human experience. Nor is there any reason to think that men and women who do not recognize that experience as their own or do not accord it the same centrality that it has for us are morally benighted. Should we press it upon them? (How would we do that?) Increased social differentiation will make it available—and supply at the same time the moral language necessary to argue about its meaning.

hibitions—of murder, deception, betrayal, gross cruelty—
that the law specifies and the police sometimes enforce.
We can, I suppose, step back, detach ourselves from our
parochial concerns, and "discover" these prohibitions. But
we can also step forward, as it were, into the thicket of
moral experience where they are more intimately known.
For they are themselves parochial concerns—concerns,
that is, of every human parish. We can, again, adopt this
or that design procedure and "invent" the prohibitions,
much as we might invent the minimally decent accommo-
dations of a hotel. But we can also study the actual historical processes by which they came to be recognized and
accepted, for they have been accepted in virtually every
human society.

These prohibitions constitute a kind of minimal and universal moral code. Because they are minimal and universal
(I should say almost universal, just to protect myself
against the odd anthropological example), they can be represented as philosophical discoveries or inventions. A single person, imagining himself a stranger, detached,
homeless, lost in the world, might well come up with
them: they are conceivable as the products of one person
talking. They are in fact, however, the products of many
people talking, of real if always tentative, intermittent, and
unfinished conversations. We might best think of them
not as discovered or invented but rather as emergent prohibitions, the work of many years, of trial and error, of
failed, partial, and insecure understandings—rather as
David Hume suggests with regard to the ban on theft (for
the sake of "stability of possession") which "arises gradually, and acquires force by a slow progression and by our
repeated experience of the inconvenience of violating it." [16]

16. Hume, *A Treatise of Human Nature,* bk. 3, pt. 2, ch. 2.

By themselves, though, these universal prohibitions barely begin to determine the shape of a fully developed or livable morality. They provide a framework for any possible (moral) life, but only a framework, with all the substantive details still to be filled in before anyone could actually live in one way rather than another. It is not until the conversations become continuous and the understandings thicken that we get anything like a moral culture, with judgment, value, the goodness of persons and things realized in detail. One cannot simply deduce a moral culture, or for that matter a legal system, from the minimal code. Both of these are specifications and elaborations of the code, variations on it. And whereas deduction would generate a single understanding of morality and law, the specifications, elaborations, and variations are necessarily plural in character.

I see no way in which the pluralism might be avoided. But if it were avoided, it would be avoided equally in morality and law; in this sense there is no difference between the two. If we had, for example, *a priori* definitions of murder, deception, and betrayal, then moral and legal specification could plausibly take shape as a series of deductive steps with a necessary end. But we do not have such definitions, and so in both cases we are dependent on socially created meanings. The moral question is general in form because it refers to the minimal code as well as to the social meanings, while the legal question is more specific because it refers only to the social meanings established in the law. But in answering the first question as much as in answering the second, our method can only be interpretive. There is nothing else to do, for the minimal code, by itself, does not answer either question.

The claim that there is nothing else to do is a stronger claim than that with which I began. We can always, I suppose, discover or invent a new and fully developed morality. It will indeed have to be fully developed if it is to reach all the way to the historically peculiar idea of human life as a career. Still, we may be tempted by discovery or invention when we see how the interpretive enterprise goes on and on, never moving toward definitive closure. Discovery and invention do not produce closure either, of course, and it is interesting to reflect for a moment on the ways in which they fail. They fail in part because there is an infinite number of possible discoveries and inventions and an endless succession of eager discoverers and inventors. But they also fail because the acceptance of a particular discovery or invention among a group of people gives rise immediately to arguments about the meaning of what has been accepted. A simple maxim: every discovery and invention (divine law is an obvious example) requires interpretation.

That is exactly right, someone might say, and it explains why interpretation is the familiar form of moral argument. It has its place and importance, but only during periods of "normal morality"—which are as workmanlike as the periods of normal science described by Thomas Kuhn—between the revolutionary, paradigm-shattering moments of discovery and invention.[17] With regard to morality, however, this view is more melodrama than realistic history. Certainly there have been historically crucial discoveries and inventions: new worlds, the force of gravity, electromagnetic waves, the power of the atom, the printing press, the steam engine, the computer, effective methods of contraception. All these have transformed the

17. Kuhn, *The Structure of Scientific Revolutions* (Chicago: University of Chicago Press, 1962).

way we live and think about the way we live. Moreover, they have done so with the force and abruptness of revelation, much as in the argument of the medieval Jewish philosopher Judah Halevi about religion: "A religion of divine origin arises suddenly. It is bidden to arise, and it is there." [18] Can we find anything like that in (secular) moral experience? The principle of utility? The rights of man? Maybe; but moral transformations seem to occur much more slowly, and less decisively, than transformations in science and technology; nor are they so clearly progressive in character as greater factual knowledge or expanded human capacities presumably are. Insofar as we can recognize moral progress, it has less to do with the discovery or invention of new principles than with the inclusion under the old principles of previously excluded men and women. And that is more a matter of (workmanlike) social criticism and political struggle than of (paradigm-shattering) philosophical speculation.

The sorts of discoveries and inventions likely to be incorporated into our moral arguments (ignoring for now discoveries and inventions that are coercively imposed) are unlikely to have definitive effects upon these arguments. We can see this in a small way in the body of literature that has grown up already around the Rawlsian difference principle, focused most importantly on the question of equality: how egalitarian would the principle actually be in its effects? And then: how egalitarian was it meant to be? how egalitarian should it be? Leave aside the deeper argument about whether the difference principle is an invention in the strong or weak sense, or even is itself an interpretation

18. Halevi, *The Kuzari*, trans. Hartwig Hirschfeld (New York: Schocken, 1964), p. 58.

or misinterpretation of our existing morality. Whatever it is, it raises questions to which there are no definitive and final answers. The difference principle may have arisen "suddenly," but it's not just "there."

Still, there are better and worse answers to the questions I have just posed, and some of the better ones will be grafted onto the principle itself and become in their turn objects of interpretation. How can we recognize the better answers? It is sometimes said against interpretation as a method in moral philosophy that we will never agree on which ones are better without the help of a correct moral theory.[19] But in the case I am now imagining, the case of the difference principle, we are driven to interpretation because we already disagree about the meaning of what purports to be, or what some readers take to be, a correct moral theory. There is no definitive way of ending the disagreement. But the best account of the difference principle would be one that rendered it coherent with other American values—equal protection, equal opportunity, political liberty, individualism—and connected it to some plausible view of incentives and productivity. We would argue about the best account, but we would know roughly what we were looking for and would have little difficulty excluding a large number of inadequate or bad accounts.

It might be helpful at this point to contrast interpretation as I understand it with Michael Oakeshott's "pursuit of intimations." His is, no doubt, an interpretive enterprise, but it is significantly constrained by the fact that Oakeshott is prepared to pursue only the intimations of

19. This is Ronald Dworkin's objection to my own *Spheres of Justice* (New York: Basic Books, 1983). See his "To Each His Own," *New York Review of Books,* April 14, 1983, pp. 4–6; the subsequent exchange, *New York Review of Books,* July 21, 1983, pp. 43–46.

"traditions of behavior" and everyday social arrangements, without any reference to "general concepts" (like
liberty or equality or, for that matter, the difference principle). The shared understandings of a people, however, are
frequently expressed in general concepts—in its historical
ideals, its public rhetoric, its foundational texts, its ceremonies and rituals. It is not only what people do but how
they explain and justify what they do, the stories they tell,
the principles they invoke, that constitute a moral culture.
Because of this, cultures are open to the possibility of contradiction (between principles and practices) as well as
to what Oakeshott calls "incoherence" (among everyday
practices). And then it is not always possible for interpretation to take the form that he prefers: "a conversation, not
an argument." Oakeshott is right to insist that "there is no
mistake-proof apparatus by means of which we can elicit
the intimations most worthwhile pursuing."[20] Indeed
there is not, but this is not to say that the pursuit might not
be (has not been) considerably more adventurous than he
allows. And in the course of the adventure, conversations
turn naturally into arguments.

Interpretation does not commit us to a positivist reading
of the actually existing morality, a description of moral
facts as if they were immediately available to our understanding. There are moral facts of that sort, but the most
interesting parts of the moral world are only in principle
factual matters; in practice they have to be "read," rendered, construed, glossed, elucidated, and not merely described. All of us are involved in doing all of these things;
we are all interpreters of the morality we share. That does

20. Oakeshott, *Rationalism in Politics* (New York: Basic Books, 1962), pp.
123–125.

not mean that the best interpretation is the sum of all the others, the product of a complicated piece of survey research—no more than the best reading of a poem is a meta-reading, summing up the responses of all the actual readers. The best reading is not different in kind, but in quality, from the other readings: it illuminates the poem in a more powerful and persuasive way. Perhaps the best reading is a new reading, seizing upon some previously misunderstood symbol or trope and re-explaining the entire poem. The case is the same with moral interpretation: it will sometimes confirm and sometimes challenge received opinion. And if we disagree with either the confirmation or the challenge, there is nothing to do but go back to the "text"—the values, principles, codes, and conventions that constitute the moral world—and to the "readers" of the text.

The readers, I suppose, are the effective authority: we hold up our interpretations for their approval.[21] But the matter is not closed if they do not approve. For readers are also rereaders who change their minds, and the population of readers also changes; we can always renew the argument. I can best explain my own view of that argument with a Talmudic story, for the Talmud is a collection of interpretations, simultaneously legal and moral in character. The background for this story is a text from Deuteronomy 30:11–14:

---

21. I mean readers in the widest sense, not only other interpreters, professionals, and adepts of one sort or another, members of what has been called the interpretive community. These people, though perhaps the most stringent readers, are only an intermediate audience. The interpretation of a moral culture is aimed at all the men and women who participate in that culture—the members of what we might call a community of experience. It is a necessary, though not a sufficient, sign of a successful interpretation that such people be able to recognize themselves in it. See also Geuss, *Idea of a Critical Theory*, pp. 64–65.

For this commandment which I command thee this day, it is not hidden from thee, neither is it far off. It is not in heaven, that thou shouldest say, Who shall go up for us to heaven, and bring it unto us, that we may hear it, and do it? Neither is it beyond the sea, that thou shouldest say, Who shall go over the sea for us, and bring it unto us, that we may hear it, and do it? But the word is very nigh unto thee, in thy mouth and in thy heart, that thou mayest do it.

I will not quote the story itself but retell it, for stories of this sort are better told than recited.[22] The story involves a dispute among a group of sages; the subject does not matter. Rabbi Eliezer stood alone, a minority of one, having brought forward every imaginable argument and failed to convince his colleagues. Exasperated, he called for divine help: "If the law is as I say, let this carob tree prove it." Whereupon the carob tree was lifted a hundred cubits in the air—some say it was lifted four hundred cubits. Rabbi Joshua spoke for the majority: "No proof can be brought from a carob tree." Then Rabbi Eliezer said, "If the law is as I say, let this stream of water prove it." And the stream immediately began to flow backward. But Rabbi Joshua said, "No proof can be brought from a stream of water." Again Rabbi Eliezer said: "If the law is as I say, let the walls of this schoolhouse prove it." And the walls began to fall. But Rabbi Joshua rebuked the walls, saying that they had no business interfering in a dispute among scholars over the moral law; and they stopped falling and to this day still stand, though at a sharp angle. And then Rabbi Eliezer called on God himself: "If the law is as I say, let it be proved from heaven." Whereupon a voice cried out,

22. Baba Metzia 59b. See also Gershom Scholem, *The Messianic Idea in Judaism* (New York: Schocken, 1971), pp. 282–303.

"Why do you dispute with Rabbi Eliezer? In all matters the law is as he says." But Rabbi Joshua stood up and exclaimed, "It is not in heaven!"

Morality, in other words, is something we have to argue about. The argument implies common possession, but common possession does not imply agreement. There is a tradition, a body of moral knowledge; and there is this group of sages, arguing. There isn't anything else. No discovery or invention can end the argument; no "proof" takes precedence over the (temporary) majority of sages.[23] That is the meaning of, "It is not in heaven." We have to continue the argument: perhaps for that reason, the story does not tell us whether, on the substantive issue, Rabbi Eliezer or Rabbi Joshua was right. On the procedural issue, however, Rabbi Joshua was exactly right. The question now is whether Rabbi Joshua, who gave up revelation, and his contemporary descendants, who have given up discovery and invention, can still say something useful, that is, something critical, about the real world.

23. Cf. a midrashic commentary on Psalm 12:7 ("The words of the Lord are . . . silver tried in the open before all men, refined seven times seven"): "Rabbi Yannai said: The words of the Torah were not given as clear-cut decisions. For with every word which the Holy One, blessed be He, spoke to Moses, He offered him forty-nine arguments by which a thing may be proved clean, and forty-nine other arguments by which it may be proved unclean. When Moses asked: Master of the universe, in what way shall we know the true sense of a law? God replied: The majority is to be followed." The majority does not make an arbitrary decision; its members search for the best of the ninety-eight arguments. *The Midrash on Psalms,* trans. William G. Braude (New Haven: Yale University Press, 1959), I, 173.

The Practice of Social Criticism

S OCIAL CRITICISM is such a common activity—so many people, in one way or another, participate in it—that we must suspect from the beginning that it does not wait upon philosophical discovery or invention. Consider the phrase itself: "social criticism" is not like "literary criticism" where the adjective tells us only the object of the enterprise named by the noun. The adjective "social" also tells us something about the subject of the enterprise. Social criticism is a social activity. "Social" has a pronominal and reflexive function, rather like "self" in "self-criticism," which names subject and object at the same time. No doubt, societies do not criticize themselves; social critics are individuals, but they are also, most of the time, members, speaking in public to other members who join in the speaking and whose speech constitutes a collective reflection upon the conditions of collective life.

This is a stipulative definition of social criticism. I do not mean to argue that it is the single possible or correct definition, only that if we imagine the dictionary's usual list, this one should come first. The opposing argument denies that reflection-from-within belongs on the list at all. For how can it ever be a satisfactory form of reflection? Don't the conditions of collective life—immediacy, closeness, emotional attachment, parochial vision—militate against a critical self-understanding? When someone says "our country," emphasizing the possessive pronoun, isn't he likely to go on to say "right or wrong?" Stephen Decatur's famous toast is often taken as an example of the sort of commitment that precludes criticism. It is not, of course, since one can still say "wrong," as Carl Schurz did in the United States Senate in 1872: "Our country, right or wrong! When right to be kept right; when wrong to be put right!" When our country behaves badly, it is still ours, and we are, perhaps, especially obligated to criticize its policies. And yet the possessive pronoun is a problem. The more closely we identify with the country, so we are commonly told, the harder it is for us to recognize or acknowledge its wrongs. Criticism requires critical distance.

It is not clear, though, how much distance critical distance is. Where do we have to stand to be social critics? The conventional view is that we have to stand outside the common circumstances of collective life. Criticism is an external activity; what makes it possible is radical detachment—and this in two senses. First, critics must be emotionally detached, wrenched loose from the intimacy and warmth of membership: disinterested and dispassionate. Second, critics must be intellectually detached, wrenched loose from the parochial understandings of their own society (standardly taken to be self-congratulatory): open-minded and objective. This view of the critic gains strength from the fact that it matches closely the conditions of philosophical discovery and invention and so seems to suggest that only discoverers or inventors, or men and women armed by discoverers or inventors, can be properly critical.

Radical detachment has the additional and not insignificant merit of turning the critic into a hero. For it is a hard business (though harder in some societies than in others) to wrench oneself loose, either emotionally or intellectually. To walk "alone . . . and in the dark" is bound to be frightening, even if one is on the road to enlightenment. Critical distance is an achievement, and the critic pays a price in comfort and solidarity. It has to be said, however, that the difficulty of finding a properly detached position is compensated for by the ease of criticism once one is there.

Not surprisingly, radical detachment does not seem to me a prerequisite of social criticism, not even of radical social criticism. It is only necessary to put together a list of critics, from the prophets of ancient Israel onward, to see how few people it actually fits. The description has become conventional in part because of a confusion between detachment and marginality. The prophets were not even marginal men, but many of their successors were. Marginality has often been a condition that motivates criticism and determines the critic's characteristic tone and appearance. It is not, however, a condition that makes for disinterest, dispassion, open-mindedness, or objectivity. Nor is it an external condition. Marginal men and women are like George Simmel's stranger, in but not wholly of their society.[1] The difficulties they experience are not the difficulties of detachment but of ambiguous connection. Free them from those difficulties, and they may well lose the reasons they have for joining the critical enterprise. Or, criticism will look very different than it looks when it is worked up on the margins by "alienated intellectuals," or members of subject classes or oppressed minorities, or even outcastes and pariahs. Now we have to imagine not a marginal critic but a critic detached from his own marginality. He might

---

1. *The Sociology of George Simmel,* trans. and ed. Kurt H. Wolff (New York: Free Press, 1950), pp. 402–408.

still be critical of any society in which groups of men and women were pushed to the margins (or he might not, seeing that the margins are so often a setting for creative activity). But his own marginality, if he remembered it, would only be a distorting factor, undercutting his capacity for objective judgment. So would his centrality, his close involvement, if he were involved, with the rulers of society. Detachment stands to the marginal and the central in exactly the same way: free of the tensions that bind the two together.

In the conventional view, the critic is not really a marginal figure; he is—he has made himself into—an outsider, a spectator, a "total stranger," a man from Mars. He derives a kind of critical authority from the distance he establishes. We might compare him to an imperial judge in a backward colony. He stands outside, in some privileged place, where he has access to "advanced" or universal principles; and he applies these principles with an impersonal (intellectual) rigor. He has no other interest in the colony except to bring it to the bar of justice. We must grant him benevolence, I suppose; he wishes the natives well. Indeed, to make the analogy tighter, he is a native himself—one of the Queen's Chinese, for example, or a westernized and Anglophile Indian, or a Parisian Marxist who happens to be Algerian. He has gone to school at the imperial center, at Paris or Oxford, say, and broken radically with his own parochialism. He would have preferred to stay at Paris or Oxford, but he has dutifully returned to his homeland so that he can criticize the local arrangements. A useful person, possibly, but not the only or the best model of a social critic.

I want to suggest an alternative model, though I do not mean to banish the dispassionate stranger or the estranged native. They have their place in the critical story, but only alongside and in the shadow of someone quite different and more familiar: the local judge, the connected critic, who earns his authority, or fails to do so, by arguing with his fellows—who, angrily and insistently, sometimes at considerable personal risk (he can be a hero too), objects, protests, and remonstrates. This critic is one of us. Perhaps he has traveled and studied abroad, but his appeal is to local or localized principles; if he has picked up new ideas on his travels, he tries to connect them to the local culture, building on his own intimate knowledge; he is not intellectually detached. Nor is he emotionally detached; he does not wish the natives well, he seeks the success of their common enterprise. This is the style of Alexander Herzen among nineteenth century Russians (despite Herzen's long exile from Russia), of Ahad Ha-am among East European Jews, of Gandhi in India, of Tawney and Orwell in Britain. Social criticism, for such people, is an internal argument. The outsider can become a *social* critic only if he manages to get himself inside, enters imaginatively into local practices and arrangements. But these critics are already inside. They see no advantage in radical detachment. If it suits their purposes, they can play at detachment, pretend to see their own society through the eyes of a stranger—like Montesquieu through the eyes of Usbek. But it is Montesquieu, the well-connected Frenchman, not Usbek, who is the social critic. Persian naiveté is a mask for French sophistication.

This alternative description fits the great majority of men and women who are plausibly called social critics. But it is not philosophically respectable. I shall try to defend its respectability by responding to two legitimate worries about the connected critic. Does his connection leave room enough for critical distance? And are standards available to him that are internal to the practices and understandings of his own society, and at the same time properly critical?

I WILL TAKE the second question first. Social criticism must be understood as one of the more important by-products of a larger activity—let us call it the activity of cultural elaboration and affirmation. This is the work of priests and prophets; teachers and sages; storytellers, poets, historians, and writers generally. As soon as these sorts of people exist, the possibility of criticism exists. It is not that they constitute a permanently subversive "new class," or that they are the carriers of an "adversary culture." They carry the common culture; as Marx argues, they do (among other things) the intellectual work of the ruling class. But so long as they do *intellectual* work, they open the way for the adversary proceeding of social criticism.

The argument that Marx first worked out in *The German Ideology* is helpful here. Marxist social criticism is based on a grand discovery—a "scientific" vision of the end of history. But this vision is only possible because the end is close at hand, its principles already apparent within bourgeois society. Criticism in other societies has been based on other visions, other principles, and Marxism is intended to provide a general account, not only of itself but of all other critical doctrines. What makes criticism a permanent possibility, according to this account, is the fact that every ruling class is compelled to present itself as a universal class.[2] There is no legitimacy in mere self-

2. Marx and Engels, *The German Ideology,* ed. R. Pascal (New York: International Publishers, 1947), pp. 40–41: "For each new class which puts itself in the

assertion. Trapped in the class struggle, seeking whatever victories are available, the rulers nevertheless claim to stand above the struggle, guardians of the common interest, their goal not victory but transcendence. This self-presentation of the rulers is elaborated by the intellectuals. Their work is apologetic, but the apology is of a sort that gives hostages to future social critics. It sets standards that the rulers will not live up to, cannot live up to, given their particularist ambitions. One might say that these standards themselves embody ruling class interests, but they do so only within a universalist disguise. And they also embody lower-class interests, else the disguise would not be convincing. Ideology strains toward universality as a condition of its success.

The Italian Marxist Antonio Gramsci provides a useful if sketchy analysis of this double embodiment. Every hegemonic culture, he argues, is a complex political construction. The intellectuals who put it together are armed with pens, not swords; they have to make a case for the ideas they are defending among men and women who have ideas of their own. "The fact of hegemony," Gramsci argues, "presupposes that one takes into account the interests and tendencies of the groups over which hegemony will be exercised, and it also presupposes a certain equilibrium, that is to say that the hegemonic groups will make some sacrifices of a corporate nature."[3] Because of these sacrifices, ruling ideas internalize contradictions, and so criticism always has a starting point inside the dominant

---

place of the one ruling before it, is compelled, merely in order to carry through its aim, to represent its interest as the common interest of all the members of society, put in an ideal form; it will give its ideas the form of universality."

3. Quoted in Chantal Mouffe, "Hegemony and Ideology in Gramsci," in Mouffe, ed., *Gramsci and Marxist Theory* (London: Routledge and Kegan Paul, 1979), p. 181.

culture. Upper-class ideology carries within itself dangerous possibilities. Gramsci's comrade in the Italian Com-
munist Party, Ignazio Silone, describes the origins of radical criticism and revolutionary politics in exactly these
terms. We begin, he writes,

> by taking seriously the principles taught us by our own educa-
> tors and teachers. These principles are proclaimed to be the
> foundations of present-day society, but if one takes them seri-
> ously and uses them as a standard to test society as it is organized
> . . . today, it becomes evident that there is a radical contradiction
> between the two. Our society in practice ignores these principles
> altogether . . . But for us they are a serious and sacred thing . . .
> the foundation of our inner life. The way society butchers them,
> using them as a mask and a tool to cheat and fool the people, fills
> us with anger and indignation. That is how one becomes a revo-
> lutionary.[4]

Gramsci himself describes a more complex process, and
one seemingly without the motivating force of indignation; it begins, however, at the same place. Radical critics
initiate, he says, "a process of differentiation and change in
the relative weight that the elements of the old ideologies
used to possess. What was previously secondary and subordinate . . . is now taken to be primary and becomes the
nucleus of a new ideological and theoretical complex."[5] So

---

4. Silone, *Bread and Wine,* trans. Gwenda David and Eric Mosbacher (New
York: Harper and Brothers, 1937), pp. 157–158. Silone's career suggests that one
ceases to be a revolutionary in the same way, by comparing the creed of the
revolutionary party to its actual practice.

5. Gramsci, *Selections from the Prison Notebooks,* ed. and trans. Quinton Hoare
and Geoffrey Nowell Smith (New York: International Publishers, 1971), p. 195.
The same argument can be made about the bourgeois creed itself. Thus Alexis de
Tocqueville on the radicals of 1789: "though they had no inkling of this, they
took over from the old regime not only most of its customs, conventions, and
modes of thought, but even those very ideas which prompted [them] to destroy
it." *The Old Regime and the French Revolution,* trans. Stuart Gilbert (Garden City,
New York: Doubleday Anchor Books, 1955), p. vii.

new ideologies emerge from old ones by way of interpretation and revision. Let us look at a concrete example.

Consider the place of equality in bourgeois and then in later critical thought. Conceived in Marxist terms as the credo of the triumphant middle classes, equality has a distinctly limited meaning. Its reference, among French revolutionaries, say, is to equality before the law, the career open to talents, and so on. It describes (and also conceals) the conditions of the competitive race for wealth and office. Radical critics delight in "exposing" its limits: it guarantees to all men and women, as Anatole France wrote, an equal right to sleep under the bridges of Paris. But the word has larger meanings—it would be less useful if it did not—subordinated within but never eliminated from the ruling ideology. These larger meanings are, to use a Gramscian term, "concessionary" in character; with them or through them the middle classes gesture toward lower-class aspiration. We are all citizens here, they claim; no one is better than anyone else. I do not mean to underestimate the sincerity of the gesture on the part of at least some of the people who make it. If it were not sincere, social criticism would have less bite than it does have. The critic exploits the larger meanings of equality, which are more mocked than mirrored in everyday experience. He condemns capitalist practice by elaborating one of the key concepts with which capitalism had originally been defended. He shows the rulers the idealized pictures their artists have painted and then the lived reality of power and oppression. Or, better, he interprets the pictures and the reality, for neither one is straightforwardly revealed. Equality is the rallying cry of the bourgeoisie; equality reinterpreted is (in the Gramscian story) the rallying cry of the proletariat.

It is entirely possible, of course, that the critic's reinterpretation will not be accepted. Perhaps the greater number of workers believe that the equality realized in capitalist society is genuine equality or that it is equality enough. Marxists call such beliefs "false consciousness"— on the assumption that equality has a single true meaning, if not for all of us then at least for the workers, namely the meaning that corresponds to their "objective" interests. I doubt that this view can be satisfactorily defended. The workers can indeed be wrong about the facts of their case, such as the actual extent of income differentials or the real chances of upward mobility. But how can they be wrong about the value and significance of equality in their own lives? Here criticism depends less on true (or false) statements about the world than on evocative (or unevocative) renderings of a common idea. The argument is about meaning and experience; its terms are set by its cultural as well as its socioeconomic setting.

But not all arguments are similarly internal. Imagine the social critic as a Marxist militant or a Christian preacher who comes (like my imperial judge) to a foreign country. There he finds natives whose conception of the world or of their own place in the world, so the newcomer believes, is radically mistaken. He measures the mistake by a wholly external standard, carried, as it were, in his luggage. If he challenges local practices, he does so in terms likely to be, at least at first, incomprehensible to the natives. Understanding waits upon conversion, and the primary task of the newcomer is a missionary task: to offer a persuasive account of a new moral or physical world. He must appear to the natives like an eagle at daybreak; they have their own owls. It is only after the new ideas have been naturalized in their new setting, woven into the fabric of the already existing culture, that native critics (or the missionary himself, if he has been naturalized, too) can put them to use. Conversion and criticism are different activities—rather like conquest and revolution. What marks off the latter terms in each of these pairs, criticism and revolution, is their partly reflexive character. In the language of the police, they are both, at their best, "inside jobs."

The newcomers might also criticize local practices in terms of what I have called the minimal code—and this sort of criticism, though it might require explanation, would presumably not require conversion. Consider the example of the Spaniards in Central America, who claimed sometimes to speak for Catholicism, sometimes only for natural law. They had, to be sure, a Catholic understanding of natural law, but they may still have been right to oppose human sacrifice, for example, not because it was contrary to orthodox doctrine but because it was "against nature." The Aztecs probably did not understand, and yet the argument did not have the same degree of externality as did arguments about the blood and body of Christ, Christian communion, and so on (and it may well have connected with the feelings, if not the convictions, of the sacrificial victims).[6] In the event, however, the naturalistic critique of human sacrifice by Spanish missionaries seems to have been largely ideological in character, a justification for external conquest, not internal reform or revolution. I

6. See Bernice Hamilton, *Political Thought in Sixteenth-Century Spain: A Study of the Political Ideas of Vitoria, De Soto, Suarez, and Molina* (Oxford: Oxford University Press, 1963), pp. 125–29. Vitoria argues that Spain has no right to enforce natural law in Central America since the Indians do not "acknowledge" any such law, but it does have a right under natural law to defend the innocent: "No one can give another man the right to kill him either for food or sacrifice. Besides, it is unquestionable that in most cases these people are killed against their wills—children for example—so it is lawful to protect them." Quoted in *Political Thought,* p. 128.

will consider a purer example of minimalist criticism in the last chapter.

If missionary work and conversion are morally necessary, if Marxism or Catholicism or any other developed creed is the only correct standard of social criticism, then correct social criticism has been impossible in most actually existing moral worlds. Nevertheless, the resources necessary for criticism of some sort, and more than a minimalist sort, are always available, because of what a moral world is, because of what we do when we construct it. The Marxist account of ideology is only one version of this construction. Another version, more familiar to contemporary philosophers, might go like this. Men and women are driven to build and inhabit moral worlds by a moral motive: a passion for justification. Sometimes only God can justify us, and then morality is likely to take shape as a conversation with God or a speculation on the standards that he might, reasonably or unreasonably, apply to our behavior. These will, in any case, be high standards, hence highly critical standards; the feeling of sin arises in part from the sense that we will never manage to live up to them.

In a secular age God is replaced by other people. Now we are driven, as Thomas Scanlon writes, by a "desire to be able to justify [our] actions to others on grounds they could not reasonably reject."[7] (We won't tolerate unreason in our peers.) It is not only rulers who want to be justified in the eyes of their subjects; each of us wants to be justified in the eyes of all the others. Scanlon suggests that this desire is triggered by the moral beliefs we already

7. Scanlon, "Contractualism and Utilitarianism," in Amartya Sen and Bernard Williams, ed., *Utilitarianism and Beyond* (Cambridge: Cambridge University Press, 1982), p. 116.

have. So it is, but it is also itself the trigger of moral belief—and then of moral argument and creativity. We try to justify ourselves, but we cannot justify ourselves by ourselves, and so morality takes shape as a conversation with particular other people, our relatives, friends, and neighbors; or it takes shape as a speculation on what arguments might, or should, persuade such people of our righteousness. Because we know the people, we can, we have to, give these arguments some specificity: they are more like "love thy neighbor" (with a suitable gloss on all three words) than "don't be indifferent to the suffering of others." They are worked out with reference to an actual, not merely a speculative, moral discourse: not one person but many people talking.

We experience morality as an external standard because it is always, necessarily, the standard of God or of other people. That is also why it is a critical standard. Just as discovered and invented moralities are critical "from the beginning"—or else there would be no cachet in discovery or invention—so our everyday morality is also critical from the beginning: it only justifies what God or other people can recognize as just. We want that recognition, even if we also want, sometimes, to do things that we know cannot be justified. Morality does not fit these other wants, though it is always possible to interpret it in a way that makes it fit. We might think of such an interpretation as the private version of an ideology. But we live anxiously with our ideologies; they are strained and awkward; they do not ring true, and we wait for some angry or indignant neighbor or friend or former friend, the private version of a social critic, to tell us so.

This account of private morality can be recapitulated at the level of collective life. Every human society provides for its members—they provide for themselves through the medium of justification—standards of virtuous character, worthy performance, just social arrangements. The standards are social artifacts; they are embodied in many different forms: legal and religious texts, moral tales, epic poems, codes of behavior, ritual practices. In all their forms they are subject to interpretation, and they are interpreted in both apologetic and critical ways. It is not the case that the apologetic interpretations are the "natural" ones, that moral standards readily fit social practices and make for smoothness and comfort, as in some functionalist utopia. The standards have to be interpreted to fit. A sustained apologetic interpretation is, again, an ideology. Since social practices, like individual practices, are morally recalcitrant, ideologies are always problematic. We know that we do not live up to the standards that might justify us. And if we ever forget that knowledge, the social critic appears to remind us. His critical interpretation is the "natural" one, given what morality is. Like Shaw's Englishman, the social critic "does everything on principle." But he is a serious, not a comic, figure because his principles are ones we share. They are only apparently external; they are really aspects of the same collective life that is perceived to require criticism. The same men and women who act badly create and sustain the standards by which (at least sometimes) they know themselves to act badly.

BUT HOW can we recognize better and worse interpretations of moral standards? The critic can, of course, get things wrong; good social criticism is as rare as good poetry or good philosophy. The critic is often passionate, obsessive, self-righteous; his hatred for the hypocrisy of his fellows may well outmeasure hypocrisy itself—"the only evil that walks / Invisible, except to God alone."[8] How can we judge the proper measure? Or again, some critical interpretations of the existing morality look backward, like Cato's; some look forward, like Marx's. Is the one way of looking better than the other? I have already suggested my own answer, or nonanswer, to such questions: they set the terms of moral argument, and the argument has no end. It has only temporary stopping points, moments of judgment. In a passive and decadent society, looking back may well be the best thing to do; in an activist and progressive society, looking forward may be the best. But then we will argue about the meaning of decadence and progress. Can't the critic step back from such endless arguments? Can't he detach himself from the conditions that make for obsession and self-righteousness? Can't he provide some objective reading of moral experience? And if he cannot do these things, might it not be better to say of him that he is angry or resentful rather than to credit him with the qualification—since it is an honorable qualification—of *critical?*

Criticism requires critical distance. But what does that mean? In the conventional view, critical distance divides the self; when we step back (mentally), we create a double. Self one is still involved, committed, parochial, angry; self two is detached, dispassionate, impartial, quietly watching self one. The claim is that self two is superior to self one, at least in this sense, that his criticism is more reliable and objective, more likely to tell us the moral truth about the world in which the critic and all the rest of us live. Self

8. John Milton, *Paradise Lost,* lines 683–684.

three would be better still. This view is plausible, at least for self two, because we have all had the experience of remembering with embarrassment, chagrin, or regret occasions on which we behaved badly. We form a certain picture of ourselves (from a distance), and the picture is painful. But this is most often a picture of ourselves as we are seen or think we are seen by people whose opinion we value. We do not look at ourselves from nowhere in particular but through the eyes of particular other people—a morally but not an epistemologically privileged position. We apply standards that we share with the others to ourselves. Social criticism works differently: we apply standards that we share with the others *to the others,* our fellow citizens, friends and enemies. We do not remember with embarrassment; we look around with anger. It may be that a critic from the ruling classes learns to see society through the eyes of the oppressed, but one of the oppressed who sees through his own eyes is no less a social critic. He will, of course, find himself caught up in arguments about what he claims to see and what he says the standards are. But he cannot win these arguments by stepping back; he can only speak again, more fully and more clearly.

The hope implicit in the conventional view is that the argument can be won once and for all. Hence that heroic figure, the perfectly disinterested spectator, imagined as a kind of all-purpose, general-service social critic. We might ask, though, why such a person would be a critic at all, rather than a radical skeptic or a mere spectator or a playful interventionist, like the Greek gods. Perhaps self one and self two do not represent different degrees of moral authority but only different orientations toward the world. Arthur Koestler makes an argument of this sort when he writes that there are "two parallel planes in our minds

which should be kept separate: the plane of detached contemplation in the sign of infinity, and the plane of action in
the name of certain ethical imperatives." Koestler believes
that the two coexist in contradiction. He bravely an-
nounces, for example, that European civilization is
doomed: "This is, so to speak, my contemplative truth.
Looking at the world with detachment . . . I find it not
even disturbing. But I also happen to believe in the ethical
imperative of fighting evil."[9] Social criticism, a matter of
ethical imperatives, clearly belongs to "the plane of action." It is curious that the plane of contemplation is so
much more melodramatic. Still, contemplative men and
women, on Koestler's reading, are not critics.

In his defense of detachment, Nagel insists that the detached observer, self two, need not be undisturbed by the
doom of civilization or by anything else happening in the
real world because he need not abandon the moral beliefs
and motivations of self one. But I do not see how he can
experience those beliefs and motivations in the same way,
once he has evacuated the moral world within which they
have their immediate reality and distanced himself from
the person for whom they are real. "When we take up the
objective standpoint," writes Nagel, as if to confirm this
skepticism, "the problem is not that values seem to disap-
pear, but that there seem to be too many of them, coming
from every life and drowning out those that arise from our
own."[10] I concede that this is still an experiencing of
values, though not quite in the common mode, and that
self two is somehow motivated to choose out of the flood
of conflicting values those that now seem to him best—

9. Koestler, *Arrow in the Blue* (New York: Stein and Day, 1984), p. 133.
10. "Limits of Objectivity," p. 115.

which may or may not be the values of self one. But would he establish any very passionate commitment to defend those values in a particular time and place? Surely one of the standard motives for detaching oneself is to escape passionate commitment (for the sake, as with Koestler, of contemplation in the sign of infinity). And if that is so, then a critic looking at society is bound to be more critical than a critic looking at himself looking at society.[11]

But there is an alternative possibility. If the effect of detachment is literally the "drowning out" of the values that arise from the critic's own life in his own time and place, then the way may be opened for an enterprise far more radical than social criticism as I have described it—an enterprise more like conversion and conquest: the total replacement of the society from which the critic has detached himself with some (imagined or actual) other. Replacement obviously depends upon the criticism of what is to be replaced. I shall not attempt a definitional exclusion: this is social criticism. It is most often, however, a morally unattractive form of social criticism and not one whose "objectivity" we should admire.

It will be useful at this point to consider, if only briefly, some historical examples. I have chosen to begin with John Locke and his well-known and rightly admired *Letter Concerning Toleration*. This is obviously a critical text, even though it was published in 1689, the year of the Toleration Act, whose principles it vindicates. The *Letter* had been written some years earlier, while Locke was living in exile

---

11. This suggests that self two would be the preferred author of a history or sociology of criticism, perhaps even of a philosophy of criticism (my own self two is writing these words). But self one is the preferred critic.

in Holland, and it was aimed at what were still the conventional views of England's political elite. Moreover, it defends a revolutionary idea; it marks a significant turning point, for Europe after the long centuries of religious persecution was a different place from Europe before. How does criticism work at moments like this?

Locke's exile might be taken as a kind of detachment from English politics, at least from established and conventional politics. Exile, we might say, is a literal enacting of critical distance. Yet Holland was hardly a realm of objectivity, and Locke's presence there did not represent anything like a philosophical "stepping back." Holland must have appeared to Locke as a (slightly) more advanced England, securely Protestant and committed to toleration. Political refugees do not escape to nowhere in particular; if they can, they choose their refuge, applying standards they already know, looking for friends and allies. So Locke's exile tied him more closely than ever before to the political forces fighting against Stuart "tyranny." It committed him to a cause. And when he defended religious toleration, he did so in terms familiar to his political associates. The *Letter* is a partisan tract, a whiggish manifesto.

But it is not only that. Locke's arguments set the terms of political discourse for the next century or more, and yet at the crucial point in the *Letter* he looks resolutely backward and invokes an idea that does not figure much in Whig politics or in the philosophies of the Enlightenment—the idea of personal salvation. Locke appeals to the meaning of salvation in Protestant thought and practice. "It is in vain," he writes, "for an unbeliever to take up the outward show of another man's profession. Faith only and inward sincerity are the things that procure acceptance with God." The *Letter* provides a particular reading, but not an idiosyncratic or outlandish reading, of Lutheran and Calvinist theology. In no sense does it call for a replacement of that theology or of the moral world of English Protestantism. Locke moves on to a powerful conclusion (which Rousseau seems to have copied and misunderstood): "Men cannot be forced to be saved whether they will or no . . . they must be left to their own consciences."[12] Locke does not speak here in the new language of natural rights; this is very much the old language of "salvation by faith alone." But his lines suggest how one might move from old to new—not so much by discovering rights as by interpreting faith, "inward sincerity," and conscience. (Hence Locke's use of rights language was not a surprise sprung on his contemporaries.) Given what salvation is, he says, or better, given what we mean by salvation (where the pronoun does not refer only to Locke's fellow exiles), persecution cannot serve the purposes claimed by its defenders. It is an injury to the moral self, also to the physical self, and nothing more.

Arguing for toleration is likely to seem to us today to be the ideal type of a dispassionate enterprise. Religious belief, so we believe, makes for passion, fanaticism, and then for persecution; toleration is the product of skepticism and disinterest. In practice, toleration is more often the product of exhaustion: all passion spent, there is nothing left but coexistence. But one can readily imagine a philosophical defense, starting from a detached observation of the folly of religious war. The theological zeal for persecution seems somehow diminished once we recognize, from a distance, the value of each and every human life. For many

---

12. Locke, *A Letter Concerning Toleration,* intro. by Patrick Romanell (Indianapolis: Bobbs-Merrill, 1950), pp. 34, 35.

seventeenth century Englishmen, however, Locke probably among them, the value of each and every human life
was closely tied to the idea of conscience, the divine spark
within each of us. Toleration was itself a theological matter, a position defended with as much zeal as any other in
the ongoing wars. Detachment might provide a (distanced) reason for endorsing that position; it does not provide a reason, or at any rate Locke's reason, for taking it
up. Indeed, an emphasis on critical distance may be a mistake here, if it leads us to miss the substantive character of
Locke's argument and to disregard its intellectual location:
within and not outside a tradition of theological discourse;
within and not above the political fray.

Opposition, far more than detachment, is what determines the shape of social criticism. The critic takes sides in
actual or latent conflicts; he sets himself against the prevailing political forces. As a result, he is sometimes driven into
exile in foreign lands or into that internal exile that we call
"alienation." It is not easy, I admit, to imagine John Locke
as an alienated intellectual; he is so central to our own
political tradition. Although he wrote anonymously on
politics and religion and thus carved out room for his own
radicalism, he nevertheless cultivated centrality, referring
himself in the *Second Treatise,* for example, to that "judi-
cious" conservative, Richard Hooker, and always inviting
readers to admire his own judiciousness. This was a matter
of prudence, no doubt, and of temperament, and of luck:
Locke's political associates were powerful men, and he
may have sensed that his exile would be, as it was, short.
Judiciousness was a wise choice. When his *Letter* was published, his friends were in power. So we need to look at
less lucky critics, whose opposition was more prolonged
and embittered. It is not the case that such people achieve

detachment—far from it—but their connection to common values and traditions of discourse is far more problematic than Locke's was. They are tempted by a kind of
leave-taking very different from that suggested by the
philosophical idea of stepping back, and different too from
Lockeian exile. They are tempted to declare a state of
war—and then to join the other side.

The easiest examples come from the history of war itself, especially from interventionist and colonial war. But
first I want to return briefly to the Marxist account of
ideology and class struggle. It is one of the major failures
of Marxism that neither Marx himself nor any of his chief
intellectual followers ever worked out a moral and political theory of socialism. Their arguments assumed a socialist future—without oppression or exploitation—but the
precise shape of that future was rarely discussed. When
Marxists wrote social criticism (rather than learned anal-
yses of the laws of capitalist development), this assumption provided a reassuring background. The force of
their criticism derived, however, from the exposure of
bourgeois hypocrisy—as in Marx's caustic comment on
English apologists for the twelve-hour working day and
the seven-day week: "and that in a country of Sabbatar-
ians!"[13] Marxists never undertook the sort of reinterpretation of bourgeois ideas that might have produced Gramsci's "new ideological and theoretical complex." The
reason for this failure lies in their view of the class struggle
as an actual war in which their task, as intellectuals, was
simply to support the workers. Implicitly, sometimes explicitly, they rejected the idea of social criticism as a collec-

---

13. Marx, *Capital*, ed. F. Engels, trans. Samuel Moore and Edward Aveling
(New York: International Publishers, 1967), I, 264.

tive reflection on collective life, because they denied the reality of collective life, of common values and a shared tradition. Even Marx's brief appeal to the idea of Sabbath rest is enough to suggest the foolishness of this denial, but the denial is nonetheless a major force within Marxism. It accounts for the essentially polemical and agitational character of the Marxist critique and the ever-present readiness to abandon "the arm of criticism" for the "criticism of arms."

In a sense, Marxists are not properly called critics of bourgeois society, for the point of their politics is not to criticize but to overthrow the bourgeoisie. They are critics of the workers instead, insofar as the workers are ideological prisoners and so fail to fulfill their historical role as the agents of overthrow. Marxists explain the failure by invoking the theory of false consciousness, which we might think of as their gesture toward common values. The theory acknowledges the commonality but treats it as a kind of collective mistake—and so misses a critical opportunity to describe socialism in socially validated and comprehensible terms. The only alternative is not to describe it at all. To discover or invent a set of socialist values does not seem to have been a practical possibility. Why should the workers stake their lives for *that?* Marx would have done better to take seriously his own metaphorical account of the new society growing in the womb of the old.

But at least Marxist writers have been fairly consistent critics of working-class ideology and then of the organization and strategy of working-class movements. There is another way of going over to the other side that abandons criticism altogether. Consider the case of Jean-Paul Sartre and the Algerian war. Sartre professed to believe that the intellectual is a permanent critic. Set loose from his own class by his search for universality, he joins the movement of the oppressed. But even here he is unassimilable: "he can never renounce his critical faculties if he is to preserve the fundamental meaning of the ends pursued by the movement." He is the "guardian of fundamental ends," which is to say, of universal values. The intellectual achieves this guardianship by a Sartrean version of "stepping back," that is, "by constantly criticizing and radicalizing [himself]." But this path to universality is a dangerous one. Having "refused" what Sartre calls his "petty bourgeois conditioning," the intellectual is likely to find himself with no concrete and substantive values at all. Universality turns out to be an empty category for deconditioned men and women, and so their commitment to the movement of the oppressed is (as Sartre at one point says it should be) "unconditional." Once committed, they are supposed to rediscover tension and contradiction: theirs is "a divided consciousness, that can never be healed."[14] In practice, however, unconditional commitment can feel like healing; at least, it can produce the symptoms of wholeness. We can see this clearly in Sartre's own life, for after he committed himself to the Algerian nationalists, he seemed incapable of a critical word about their principles or policies. Henceforth he aimed his ideas, as a soldier with more justification might aim his gun, in only one direction.

Of course, Sartre was a critic, and a consistent and brave critic, of French society—of the Algerian war and then of the conduct of the war, both of these viewed as necessary consequences of French colonialism. But since he de-

---

14. Sartre, *Between Existentialism and Marxism,* trans. John Mathews (New York: Pantheon, 1983), p. 261.

scribed himself as an enemy and even a "traitor," as if, with characteristic hauteur, to accept the charge of his right-wing foes, he cut the ground from under his own enterprise.[15] An enemy is not recognizable as a social critic; he lacks standing. We expect and simultaneously discount criticism from our enemies. And the discount is especially easy if the criticism is made in the name of "universal" principles that are applied only to us. But perhaps we should think of Sartre's self-description, and of his elaborate account of the critic's "role," as a kind of theoretical smokescreen behind which he and his friends engaged in a familiar politics of internal opposition. Certainly the principles he applied were well known in France; that, indeed, is where the leaders of the Algerian nationalists had learned them. French intellectuals hardly had to step back or subject themselves to self-criticism in order to discover, say, the idea of self-determination. The idea was already theirs; they had only to apply it—that is, to extend its application to Algeria. What prevented Sartre from adopting this view of his own activity was his conception of criticism as war. The war was real enough, but the critique of the war was a distinct and separate enterprise. Join the two, and the critique is, as it was in Sartre's case, corrupted.

There are, then, two extremes (the description is convenient if inexact): philosophical detachment and a "treason-

15. Cf. the words of an even more hard-pressed critic of his own society, the Afrikaner writer André Brink: "If the Afrikaner dissident today encounters such a vicious reaction from the Establishment, it is because he is regarded as a traitor to everything Afrikanerdom stands for (since apartheid has usurped for itself that definition)—whereas, in fact, the dissident is fighting to assert the most positive and creative aspects of his heritage." *Writing in a State of Siege: Essays on Politics and Literature* (New York: Summit Books, 1983), p. 19. Brink is a connected critic, but this is not to deny that he might one day be driven into physical exile or even into a kind of moral exile, as it were, beyond his brave "whereas."

ous" engagement, stepping back and going over. The first is a precondition of the second; undercommitment to one's own society makes, or can make, for overcommitment to some theoretical or practical other. The proper ground of social criticism is the ground that the detached philosopher and the Sartrean "traitor" have alike abandoned. But does this ground allow for critical distance? It obviously does, else we would have far fewer critics than we do. Criticism does not require us to step back from society as a whole but only to step away from certain sorts of power relationships within society. It is not connection but authority and domination from which we must distance ourselves. Marginality is one way of establishing (or experiencing) this distance; certain sorts of internal withdrawal provide other ways. I am inclined to think that something like this is a requirement of intellectual life generally, as in the advice given by a Talmudic sage to would-be sages: "Love work, do not domineer over others, and never seek the intimacy of public officials." [16] The actual wielding of power and the Machiavellian ambition to whisper in the ear of the prince: these are real obstacles to the practice of criticism, because they make it difficult to look with open eyes at those features of society most in need of critical scrutiny. But opposition is not a similar obstacle, though we are no more objective in opposition than in power.

Think for a moment of critical distance in the caricatured and slightly comic categories of age. The old are critics rather as Cato was, who believe that things have gone steadily downhill since their youth. The young are critics rather as Marx was, who believe that the best is yet to be. Age and youth both make for critical distance; the uncritical years presumably come in between. But the

16. *Pirke Avot* (Sayings of the Fathers), 1.10.

principles of the old and the young are not distant, and they are certainly not objective. The old remember a time that is not so long ago. The young are newly socialized: if they are also (sometimes) radical and idealistic, this says something about the intellectual content of socialization. What makes criticism possible, or relatively easy, for both of these groups is a certain quality of not being involved, or not fully involved, in the local forms of getting and spending, not being responsible for what happens, not being politically in control. The old may have relinquished control reluctantly; the young may be eager to win it. But willingly or not, both groups stand a little to the side. They are, or they can be, kibitzers.

A little to the side, but not outside: critical distance is measured in inches. Though old and young are not in control of the major economic or political enterprises of their society, they are also not without some commitment to the success of those enterprises, at least to their eventual success. They want things to go well. This is also the common stance of the social critic. He is not a detached observer, even when he looks at the society he inhabits with a fresh and skeptical eye. He is not an enemy, even when he is fiercely opposed to this or that prevailing practice or institutional arrangement. His criticism does not require either detachment or enmity, because he finds a warrant for critical engagement in the idealism, even if it is a hypocritical idealism, of the actually existing moral world.

BUT THIS is a picture of the social critic as he commonly is; it is not a picture of the ideal social critic. I confess that I cannot imagine such a person—not, at least, if we have to imagine him as a single type of person, with a single (objective) standpoint and a single set of critical principles. Nevertheless, I have managed to smuggle into my picture a certain idealism of my own, which is different from the local and various idealisms of actual social critics. I have, not at all surreptitiously, attached value to the critic's connection to his own society. But why should connection be generally valuable, given that societies are so different? Criticism works best, of course, if the critic is able to invoke local values, but it is not the case that criticism does not work at all if the critic is not able or does not want to do that. Consider the case of the Bolshevik intellectuals in Russia, which Gramsci has summed up in a nice couple of sentences:

> An elite consisting of some of the most active, energetic, enterprising and disciplined members of the society emigrates abroad and assimilates the cultural and historical experiences of the most advanced countries of the West, without however losing the most essential characteristics of its own nationality, that is to say without breaking its sentimental and historical ties with its own people. Having thus performed its intellectual apprenticeship it returns to its own country and compels the people to an enforced awakening, skipping historical stages in the process.[17]

The reference to "sentimental ties" is necessary to explain why these enterprising intellectuals, having assimilated Western culture, did not just remain in the West. They saw the sun but nevertheless went back to the cave. Once back, however, they apparently were not animated much by sentiment. They had brought with them a great discovery—more scientific than moral in character—for the sake of which they had traveled a great distance, not only in space: they had also gone forward in time (far more so

17. *Prison Notebooks*, pp. 19–20.

than Locke in Holland). Theoretical advancement was the form of their detachment from Old Russia. Now they confronted Russia with a true doctrine that had no Russian roots. Bolshevik social criticism draws heavily, to be sure, on Russian circumstances and arguments. It was necessary, Lenin wrote, "to collect and utilize every grain of even rudimentary protest," and rudimentary protest, unlike doctrinal discovery, is always a local phenomenon.[18] But this kind of criticism was crudely instrumental in character. The Bolshevik leaders made no serious effort to connect themselves to the common values of Russian culture. And that is why, once they had seized power, they were compelled to "compel the people to an enforced awakening."

I am tempted to say of Lenin and his friends that they were not social critics at all, since what they wrote was narrowly analytical in character or narrowly agitational. But it is probably better to say that they were bad social critics, looking at Russia from a great distance and merely disliking what they saw. Similarly, they were bad revolutionaries, for they seized power through a *coup d'état* and ruled the country as if they had conquered it. The group of Russian radicals who called themselves Social Revolutionaries makes for a useful comparison. The Social Revolutionaries labored hard to recover the communal values of the Russian village and so to construct a Russian argument against the new rural capitalism. They told a story about the *mir*. I suspect that this story, like most such stories, was largely fanciful. The values, though, were real, that is, recognized and accepted by many Russians, even if they

18. Lenin, *What Is To Be Done?* (Moscow: Foreign Languages Publishing House, 1947), p. 101.

were not—even if they had never been—institutionally embodied. And so the Social Revolutionaries developed a critique of social relations in the Russian countryside that had some (I don't want to exaggerate) richness, detail, and nuance, and which was comprehensible to the people whose relations those were. The Bolsheviks, by contrast, were either incomprehensible or insincere, moving erratically back and forth between Marxist theory and an opportunistic politics.

The problem with disconnected criticism, and thus with criticism that derives from newly discovered or invented moral standards, is that it presses its practitioners toward manipulation and compulsion. Many, of course, resist the pressure; detachment and dispassion are built-in defenses against it. But insofar as the critic wants to be effective, wants to drive his criticism home (though the home is, in a sense, no longer his own), he finds himself driven to one or another version of an unattractive politics. It is for this reason that I have tried to distinguish his enterprise from collective reflection, criticism from within, or as it is sometimes called, "immanent critique." His is a kind of asocial criticism, an external intervention, a coercive act, intellectual in form but pointing toward its physical counterpart. Perhaps there are some societies so closed in upon themselves, so rigidly confined even in their ideological justifications, that they require asocial criticism; no other kind is possible. Perhaps—but it is my own belief that such societies are more likely to be found in social science fiction than in the real world.[19]

19. It is easier to think of subgroups within larger societies that might meet this description, such as tightly knit orthodox religious communities like the Amish or Hasidic Jews in the United States today. Orthodoxy itself is no bar to internal criticism, as the endless heresies of medieval Christendom or the dissi-

Sometimes, though, even in the real world, the critic is driven into a kind of asociability, not because he has discovered new moral standards but because he has discovered a new theology or cosmology or psychology, unknown, even outrageous, to his fellows, from which moral arguments seem to follow. Freud is the best modern example. His critique of sexual morality might have been based, as similar critiques were later based, on liberal ideas of freedom and individuality. Freud argued instead from his newly discovered psychological theory. He was indeed a great discoverer, an eagle among discoverers, and then a heroic critic of repressive laws and practices. And yet a Freudian or therapeutic politics would be as unattractive, as manipulative, as any other politics founded on discovery and disconnected from local understandings. It is a good thing, then, that neither criticism nor oppositional politics depends upon discoveries of this sort. Social criticism is less the practical offspring of scientific knowledge than the educated cousin of common complaint. We become critics naturally, as it were, by elaborating on existing moralities and telling stories about a society more just than, though never entirely different from, our own.

It is better to tell stories—better even though there is no definitive and best story, better even though there is no last story that, once told, would leave all future storytellers without employment. I understand that this indeterminacy prompts, not without reason, a certain philosophical

---

dence of dissent among Protestants clearly suggest. But the smaller and more beleaguered the community, the less likely it is to offer resources to the connected critic. He will have to appeal to some wider political or religious tradition within which his own is (uneasily) located—as a critic of Amish or Hasidic society might appeal to Protestantism or Judaism more generally or to American liberalism.

apprehension. And from this there follows the whole elaborate apparatus of detachment and objectivity, whose purpose is not to facilitate criticism but to guarantee its correctness. The truth is that there is no guarantee, any more than there is a guarantor. Nor is there a society, waiting to be discovered or invented, that would not require our critical stories.

The Prophet as Social Critic

T HE CONTRASTS and contradictions that I have so far discussed—discovered or invented morality, on the one hand, and interpreted morality, on the other; external and internal criticism; shared values and everyday practices; social connection and critical distance—all these are very old. They are not the property of the modern age; though I have described them in what is undoubtedly a modern idiom, they have in other times and places been described in other idioms. They are fully visible in the very earliest examples of social criticism, and I want in this last chapter to see how they look in what may well have been their first appearance, at least in Western history. It is time to add historical flesh to the theoretical bones of my argument. And how better to prove that the connected critic is flesh of our flesh than to give him the name of Amos, the first and possibly the most radical of Israel's literary prophets?

I shall try to understand and explain the practice of prophecy in ancient Israel. I do not mean the personality of the prophet; I am not interested in the psychology of inspiration or of ecstasy. Nor do I mean the prophetic texts; these are painfully obscure at many points, and I do not possess the historical or philological knowledge necessary to decipher them (or even to offer speculative readings of disputed passages). I want to understand prophecy as a social practice: not the men or the texts but the message, and also the reception of the message. Of course, there were prophets before the ones we know, seers and soothsayers, oracles, diviners, and clairvoyants; and there is nothing very puzzling about their messages or about their audiences. Foretellings of doom and glory will always find listeners, especially when the doom is for enemies, the glory for ourselves. The people say, according to Isaiah, "Speak unto us smooth things" (30:10), and that is what the professional prophets of courts and temples commonly do.[1] It is only when these foretellings are set, as Amos first sets them, within a moral frame, when they are an occasion for indignation, when prophecies are also provocations, verbal assaults on the institutions and activities of everyday life, that they become interesting. Then it is a puzzle why people listen, and not only listen but copy down, preserve, and repeat the prophetic message. The message is not a smooth one; it cannot be happily heard or readily followed; the people, most of them, do not do what the prophet urges them to do. But they choose to remember his urging. Why?

It is here, writes Max Weber, "that the demagogue appears for the first time in the records of history." But that is not quite right, for though the prophets spoke to the people and, arguably, on their behalf, and though they spoke with the fierceness and anger we conventionally attribute to demagogues, they do not seem to have sought a popular following or ever to have aspired to political office. Weber is closer to the truth when he argues that the prophecies, written down and circulated in the cities of

1. See Johannes Lindblom, *Prophecy in Ancient Israel* (Oxford: Basil Blackwell, 1962), chs. 1–2; Joseph Blenkensopp, *A History of Prophecy in Israel* (London: SPCK, 1984), ch. 2.

Israel and Judah, represent the earliest known example of the political pamphlet.[2] But that suggestion is too narrow. Prophetic religion embraced not only politics but every aspect of social life. The prophets were (the term is only mildly anachronistic) social critics. Indeed, they were the inventors of the practice of social criticism, though not of their own critical messages. And so we can learn from reading them and studying their society something about the conditions that make criticism possible and give it force, and something too about the place and standing of the critic among the people he criticizes.

THE FIRST thing to notice is that the prophetic message depends upon previous messages. It is not something radically new; the prophet is not the first to find, nor does he make, the morality he expounds. We can detect a certain theological revisionism in some of the later prophets, but none of them presents an entirely original doctrine. For the most part, they disclaim originality, and not only in the obvious sense that they attribute their message to God. It is more important that they continually refer themselves to the epic history and the moral teaching of the Torah: "He hath showed thee, O man, what is good" (Micah 6:8). The past tense is significant. The prophets assume the previous messages, the divine "showings," the immediacy of history and law in the minds of their listeners. They have no esoteric teaching, not even for their closest disciples. They speak to a large audience, and for all their anger, they seem to take that audience for granted. They assume, writes

2. Weber, *Ancient Judaism,* trans. H. H. Gerth and Don Martindale (Glencoe: Free Press, 1952), pp. 268–269, 272.

Johannes Lindblom, "that their words could be immediately understood and accepted"—not, however, that
they would be: they knew the people for whom they
prophesied.[3]

The prophetic assumption finds its sociological correlate
in the political and communal structure of ancient Israel: a
loose, localized, and conflict-ridden set of arrangements
that stood at some distance from the unified hierarchies of
Egypt to the west and Assyria to the east. In Israel, religion
was not the exclusive possession of priests, and law was
not the exclusive possession of royal bureaucrats.
Prophecy in the form we know it, in critical form, would
not have been possible except for the relative weakness of
priesthood and bureaucracy in the everyday life of the
country. The necessary background conditions are indi-
cated in the prophetic texts: justice is done (or not done) in
the "gates" of the city, and religion is discussed in the
streets.[4] The Bible clearly suggests the existence among
the Israelites of a strong lay and popular religiosity. This
had two aspects, individual piety and a more or less common, though fiercely disputed, covenantal creed. Taken
together, the two made for a culture of prayer and argument that was independent of the more formal religious
culture of pilgrimage and sacrifice. Sustained no doubt, as
Weber says, by "circles of urban intellectuals," this informal religiosity also reached beyond such circles.[5] Had it
not done so, the prophet would never have found his audience.

Or prophecy would have taken a wholly different form.

3. *Prophecy in Ancient Israel,* p. 313.
4. See James Luther May, *Amos: A Commentary* (Philadelphia: Westminster,
1969), pp. 11, 93.
5. *Ancient Judaism,* p. 279.

I will try to illustrate one alternative possibility out of the book of Jonah, a tale about a prophet sent by God to the city of Nineveh, where the appeal to Israel's history and law would obviously make no sense. But first I need to say something more about the conditions under which the appeal does make sense, especially about the strength and legitimacy of lay religion. In part, this is a matter of popular practices, like the practice of spontaneous prayer that Moshe Greenberg has described.[6] But there is also what we might call an idea or even a doctrine of lay religiosity. The doctrine is entirely appropriate to a covenantal creed, and it is most clearly set forth in Deuteronomy, the crucial exposition of Israel's covenant theology. The precise relation of Deuteronomy to the prophetic movement is a subject of debate. Did the prophets influence the Deuteronomic writers, or the writers the prophets? It seems likely that the influence worked in both directions and in ways that we shall never wholly understand. In any case, a large number of passages in the prophetic books echo (or anticipate?) the Deuteronomic text as we now have it, and the covenantal tradition that Deuteronomy elaborates is surely older than Amos, though the "discovery" of the text did not take place until a century and a half after Amos's prophecies.[7] So I shall take the book to suggest the doctrinal background of prophecy: a normative account of the informal and unpriestly culture of prayer and argument.

I want to look briefly at two passages, the first from the end of Deuteronomy, the second from the beginning.

---

6. Greenberg, *Biblical Prose Prayer as a Window to the Popular Religion of Ancient Israel* (Berkeley: University of California Press, 1983).

7. See Anthony Phillips, "Prophecy and Law," in R. Coggins, A. Phillips, and M. Knibb, ed., *Israel's Prophetic Tradition* (Cambridge: Cambridge University Press, 1982), p. 218.

Whether either of these was part of the manuscript that turned up in Jerusalem in the year 621 B.C.E., I cannot say, nor can anyone else. But they share the spirit of the original as a covenantal document. The first passage formed the basis of the Talmudic story with which I concluded the first chapter:

> For this commandment which I command thee this day, it is not hidden from thee [Hebrew: *felah,* alternatively translated "it is not too hard for thee"]; neither is it far off. It is not in heaven, that thou shouldest say, Who shall go up for us to heaven, and bring it unto us, that we may hear it, and do it? Neither is it beyond the sea . . . But the word is very nigh unto thee, in thy mouth, and in thy heart, that thou mayest do it.   *(Deut. 30:11–14)*

Moses indeed climbed the mountain, but no one need do that again. There is no longer any special role for mediators between the people and God. The law is not in heaven; it is a social possession. The prophet need only show the people their own hearts. If his is a "voice in the wilderness" (Isaiah 40:3), it is not because he has embarked on a heroic quest for God's commandments. The image recalls the history of the people themselves, their own wilderness time, when God's voice was the voice in the wilderness, and reminds them that they already know the commandments. And though they may need to be reminded, the knowledge is readily renewed, for the Torah is not an esoteric teaching. It is not hidden, obscure, difficult (the Hebrew word has all these meanings, as well as "marvelous" and "set aside," as a sacred text might be set aside for a body of specially trained priests). The teaching is available, common, popular—so much so that everyone is commanded to speak about it:

And these words which I command thee this day shall be in thine heart: And thou shalt teach them diligently unto thy children, and shalt talk of them when thou sittest in thine house, and when thou walkest by the way, and when thou liest down and when thou risest up.   *(Deut. 6:6–7)*

Prophecy is a special kind of talking, not so much an educated as an inspired and poetic version of what must have been at least sometimes, among some significant part of the prophet's audience, ordinary discourse. Not only ritual repetition of key texts but heartfelt prayer, storytelling, and doctrinal debate: the Bible provides evidence for all of this, and prophecy is continuous with it, dependent upon it. Though there is conflict between the prophets and the established priesthood, prophecy does not in any sense constitute an underground or a sectarian movement. In the dispute between Amos and the priest Amaziah, it is the prophet who appeals to religious tradition, the priest only to reason of state (7:10–17). Prophecy aims to arouse remembrance, recognition, indignation, repentence. In Hebrew, the last of these words derives from a root meaning "to turn, to turn back, to return," and so it implies that repentance is parasitic upon a previously accepted and commonly understood morality. The same implication is apparent in prophecy itself. The prophet foretells doom, but what motivates his listeners is not only fear of coming disasters but also knowledge of the law, a sense of their own history, and a feeling for the religious tradition. Prophetic admonition, writes Greenberg,

presupposes common ground on which prophet and audience stand, not only regarding historical traditions but religious demands as well. The prophets seem to appeal to their audience's better nature, confronting them with demands of God that they know (or knew) but wish to ignore or forget . . . There is more than a little optimism underlying the generations-long succession of reforming prophets; it reflects the prophets' confidence that, in the final analysis, they had advocates in the hearts of their audience.[8]

CONTRAST this view with the example provided by the book of Jonah. This is a late (postexilic) tale commonly taken to argue for the universalism of divine law and divine concern, though universalism is in fact an ancient argument. Perhaps Jonah is an ancient tale, retold sometime after the return from Babylonia as an attack upon the parochialism of the Judean restoration. The immediate issue of the story is the reversibility of divine decree, an issue raised, at least implicitly, in the earliest prophets.[9] That God himself is capable of "repentance" is suggested by Amos (7:3), and there is a striking example even earlier, in the Exodus story. But I want to stress another feature of the book of Jonah and contrast the content of Jonah's message with that of the prophets in Israel. The contrast would be sharper if the Jonah of the tale could be identified with the prophet Jonah, son of Amitai, mentioned in 2 *Kings* 14:25, a contemporary of Amos, but it does not depend upon the identification. For my immediate purposes the provenance of the tale and its author's intentions matter less than the tale itself. I shall take the "plot" literally and pass over its obvious ironies (the fact, for ex-

8. *Prose Prayer,* p. 56.
9. Yehezkel Kaufmann, *The Religion of Israel,* trans. Moshe Greenberg (Chicago: University of Chicago Press, 1960), pp. 282–284, argues that the book of Jonah as we have it dates from the eighth century B.C.E., but few scholars agree with him.

ample, that the Ninevans actually repented, while none of Israel's own prophets could report a similar success). When Jonah prophesies doom in Nineveh, he is necessarily a different sort of prophet from Amos in Beth-El or Micah in Jerusalem—for doom is the entire content of his prophecy. He cannot refer to a religious tradition or a moral law embodied in covenantal form. Whatever the religion of the inhabitants of Nineveh, Jonah appears to know nothing about it and to take no interest in it. He is a detached critic of Ninevan society, and his prophecy is a single sentence: "Yet forty days and Nineveh shall be overthrown" (3:4).

"Overthrown" is the verb used in Genesis 19:25 to describe the fate of Sodom and Gomorrah, and it serves to assimilate Nineveh to these two cities. All three are condemned because of the "wickedness" of their inhabitants. Nahum Sarna suggests a further comparison, based on another repeated word. Nineveh is charged with the crime of "violence," echoing the charge that explains the flood: "and the earth was filled with violence" (Genesis 6:11). In neither case is anything more specific said.[10] Sodom's wickedness is at least minimally specified: its immediate form is the sexual mistreatment of guests and strangers. But we actually know very little about the internal life of Sodom or the moral history or commitments of its citizens. And we know even less about the world before the flood or about the faraway city of Nineveh. Jonah tells us nothing at all: this is prophecy without poetry, without resonance, allusion, or concrete detail. The prophet comes and goes, an alien voice, a mere messenger, unconnected

---

10. Nahum Sarna, *Understanding Genesis: The Heritage of Biblical Israel* (New York: Schocken, 1970), p. 145.

to the people of the city. Even the regard for the people that God teaches him at the end is only a rather abstract "pity" for the "six score thousand persons that cannot discern between their right hand and their left hand" (4:11).

This last phrase probably refers to the children of Nineveh; the adults, it appears, have some discernment, for they do repent. Though Jonah does not say anything about it, there is some moral knowledge to which they can return, some basic understanding that God and his prophet alike presuppose. Of course, Nineveh has its own moral and religious history, its own creed, its own code, its own shrines and priests—its own gods. But it is not Jonah's purpose to remind the people of what is their own; only a local prophet (a connected critic) could do that. Try to imagine Jonah in conversation with the Ninevans: what could he have said? Conversation is parasitic on commonality, and since commonality is minimal here, we can imagine only a minimal conversation. It is not that there is nothing at all to say, but the talk would be thin, centered on those moral understandings that do not depend upon communal life; there would be little room for nuance or subtlety. Thus Jonah's prophecy, and his achievement: the people recognize and turn away "from the violence that is in their hands" (3:8). What is this "violence" whose recognition does not depend upon a particular moral or religious history?

The first two chapters of the book of Amos provide an answer to this question. Here the prophet "judges" a group of nations with which Israel has recently been at war, and he provides a brief, though sometimes obscure, account of their crimes. Damascus "threshed Gilead with sledges of iron"—a reference, apparently, to extreme cruelty in warfare; Gaza "carried away captive a whole captivity"; Tyre violated a treaty; Edom pursued "his brother with the sword, and did cast off all pity"; Ammon "ripped up the women with child of Gilead"; Moab burned the bones of the king of Edom, denying him honorable burial (1:3–2:2). All these are crimes of "violence," and in all of them the victims are enemies and strangers, not fellow citizens. These are the only crimes for which the "nations" (in contrast to Israel and Judah) are punished. The prophet judges Israel's neighbors only for violations of a minimal code, "a form of international religious law," Weber suggests, "presupposed as valid among the Palestine peoples."[11] Of the substantive social morality of these peoples, their domestic practices and institutions, Amos, like Jonah in Nineveh, has nothing to say.

Amos's judgment of the nations suggests not a late and innovative but an early and familiar universalism. The existence of a kind of international law, fixing the treatment of enemies and strangers, seems to be presupposed in the story of Sodom and Gomorrah, to which Amos refers casually as if his audience knows it well (4:11), and some such minimal code may also underlie the story of the flood. The author of the book of Jonah, centuries later, adds nothing to the argument. God will punish "violence" wherever it occurs. But alongside this universalism there is a more particularist message, delivered only (at least by Israelite prophets) to the children of Israel:

> You only have I known of all the families of the earth;
> Therefore I will visit upon you all your iniquities.   *(3:2)*

"All your iniquities," domestic as well as international: the elaboration of this phrase constitutes the particular morality, the substantive argument of the prophets.

---

11. *Ancient Judaism*, p. 302.

THE CONCERN of the prophets is for *this* people, their own people, the "family," as Amos says, that came up out of Egypt (2:10). (For my present purposes I will ignore the political division between the rival kingdoms of Israel and Judah; the two share a history and a law, and prophets like Amos go back and forth between them.) Jonah, by contrast, has no personal interest in Nineveh and no knowledge of its moral history. Hence Martin Buber is wrong to call the Jonah story a "paradigm of the prophetic nature and task."[12] The paradigmatic task of the prophets is to judge the people's relations with one another (and with "their" God), to judge the internal character of their society, which is exactly what Jonah does not do. Prophetic teaching, writes Lindblom more accurately, "is characterized by the principle of solidarity. Behind the demand for charity and justice . . . lies the idea of the *people,* the people as an organic whole, united by election and covenant"— singled out, we might say, by a peculiar history.[13] Committed to this solidarity, the prophets avoid sectarianism just as they avoid any larger universalism. They attempt no further singling out; they make no effort to gather around themselves a band of "brethren." When they address their audience, they always use inclusive proper names—Israel, Joseph, Jacob; their focus is always on the fate of the covenanted community as a whole.

For the same reason, the message of the prophets is resolutely this-worldly. Theirs is a social and workaday ethic. Two points are crucial here, both of which I take from Weber, whose comparative perspective is especially illuminating.[14] First, there is no prophetic utopia, no ac-

---

12. Buber, *The Prophetic Faith* (New York: Harper and Brothers, 1960), p. 104.
13. *Prophecy in Ancient Israel,* p. 344.
14. *Ancient Judaism,* pp. 275, 285, 313–314.

count (in the style of Plato, say) of the "best" political or
religious regime, a regime free from history, located any-
where or nowhere. The prophets do not have philosophical imaginations. They are rooted, for all their anger, in
their own societies. The house of Israel is here, and it needs
only to be ordered in accordance with its own laws. Second, the prophets take no interest in individual salvation
or in the perfection of their own souls. They are not religious adepts or mystics; they never advocate asceticism or
world rejection. Wrongdoing and rightdoing are alike
social experiences, and the prophet and his listeners are
involved in these experiences in accordance with the principle of solidarity, whether or not any given right or
wrong act is their own. Utopian speculation and world
rejection are two forms of escape from particularism. The
two always take culturally specific forms, but they are in
principle available without regard to cultural identity: anyone can leave the world behind, anyone can come to "nowhere." The prophetic argument, by contrast, is that this
people must live in this way.

The prophets invoke a particular religious tradition and
a particular moral law, both of which they assume their
audience to know. The references are constant, and while
some of them are mysterious to us, they were presumably
not mysterious to the men and women who gathered at
Beth-El or Jerusalem to listen. We need footnotes, but
prophecy is not, like some modern poetry, meant to be
read with footnotes. Consider these lines from Amos,
which follow close upon the famous passage about sell-
ing the righteous for silver and the needy for a pair of
shoes:

> And they lay themselves down beside every altar
> Upon clothes taken in pledge. *(2:8)*

The reference here is to the law of Exodus 22:26–27 (part of the Book of the Covenant): "If thou at all take thy neighbor's raiment to pledge, thou shalt deliver it unto him by the time the sun goeth down: For that is his covering only, it is his raiment for his skin: wherein shall he sleep?" The prophet's complaint makes no sense without the law. Whether the law was already written down (as seems likely in this case) or known only through an oral tradition, the point is that it was known and, judging from the form of the reference, commonly known. Yet neither the law nor the morality behind the law is universally known. We have different ideas about the pledge (the pawn), and it is not obvious that our ideas are unjust.

But the prophets do not only recall and repeat the tradition, they also interpret and revise it. I have sometimes encountered efforts to deny the value of the prophetic example for a general understanding of social criticism by arguing that Israel possessed an unusually coherent moral tradition, whereas we today have only competing traditions and endless disagreements.[15] But the coherence of Israelite religion is more a consequence than a precondition of the work of the prophets. Their prophecies, together with the writings of the Deuteronomic school, begin the creation of something we might call normative Judaism. It is important to stress the pre-existing moral and legal

---

15. Alternatively, it is pointed out that Amos can speak in the name of God, whereas we can claim no such authority. This makes a difference, of course, but not of a relevant kind. Criticism is an adversarial proceeding, and the relevant comparison is between the critic and his adversary, not between critics from one culture and critics from another. And Amos's adversaries also spoke in God's name, while the adversaries of contemporary social critics usually make no such claim. What is similar across cultures is the similarity within cultures: the same resources—authoritative texts, memories, values, practices, conventions—are available to social critics and to defenders of the *status quo*.

codes, the sense of a common past, the depth of popular religiosity. But all this was still theologically inchoate, highly contentious, radically pluralistic in form. In fact, the prophets pick and choose among the available materials. What priests like Amaziah take to be "secondary and subordinate" in Israelite religion, the prophets take "to be primary . . . the nucleus of a new . . . theoretical complex." Or to put the same point differently, the prophets try to work up a picture of the tradition that will make sense to, and connect with the experience of, their own contemporaries. They are parasitic upon the past, but they also give shape to the past upon which they are parasitic.[16]

Even here, they probably do not act alone. Just as we need to resist the portrayal of ancient Israel as a special case of moral coherence, so we need to resist the portrayal of the prophets as peculiar, eccentric, and lonely individuals. They are no more alone when they interpret the Israelite creed than when they repeat the creed. Interpretation as I have described it, as the prophets practiced it, is a common activity. The new emphasis upon the social code of Exodus, for example, is almost certainly rooted in discussions and arguments that went on—they are easy to imagine—in the cities of Israel and Judah. Amos can hardly have been the first person to realize that the law of the

16. Walther Zimmerli argues that the prophets break far more radically with the past than this last paragraph suggests. The prophetic "proclamation" overwhelms, even as it exploits, traditional material and therefore cannot be captured under the rubric of "interpretation." Tradition "in the salutary sense of the term, shatters and becomes an empty shell of mere historical recollection." "Prophetic Proclamation and Reinterpretation," in Douglas Knight, ed., *Tradition and Theology in the Old Testament* (Philadelphia: Fortress Press, n.d.), p. 99. But this ignores the content of the prophetic proclamation, the terms or standards to which Israel is held. Judgment would be entirely arbitrary if it did not refer to standards with which the people were, or were supposed to be, familiar. Amos makes that reference systematically.

pledge was being violated. He speaks against a back-ground of urban growth and class differentiation that gave that law, and all the Exodus laws, a new relevance. Simi-larly, the prophetic de-emphasis of ritual sacrifice is rooted in popular piety, in the rejection or avoidance of priestly mediation, in a spontaneous acting out, through individual prayer, of the ancient dream that all Israel would be "a kingdom of priests and a holy nation."[17] Still, it is the prophets who most clearly establish the link between piety and conduct and who most explicitly use the Exodus laws as a weapon of social criticism.

The argument of Amos dramatically displays both the new emphasis and the new de-emphasis. We must assume the social changes that precede and motivate his prophecy: the introduction of greater and greater inequalities into what had been, and still was ideally, an association of freemen. No doubt, inequality of some sort was already ancient, else there would have been no ancient social code aimed at ameliorating its effects. But by the eighth century B.C.E., the years of monarchic rule had produced in and around the court and in the growing cities a new upper class feeding on a new lower class. Archaeological finds, more explicit in this case than they usually are, confirm the development: "the simple, uniform houses of the earlier centuries had been replaced by luxurious dwellings of the rich on the one hand, by hovels on the other."[18] Amos is, above all, a critic of this new upper class, whose members were increasingly capable of and committed to what we now call a high standard of living, with winter houses and

---

17. Greenberg, *Prose Prayer,* p. 52.
18. Martin Smith, *Palestinian Parties and Politics That Shaped the Old Testament* (New York: Columbia University Press, 1971), p. 139.

summer houses (3:5), couches of ivory (6:4), sumptuous feasts, and costly perfumes:

> That drink wine in bowls
> And anoint themselves with the chief ointments. *(6:6)*

The prophet's caustic description of all this is often characterized as a kind of rural puritanism, the dislike of a countryman for city fanciness.[19] Perhaps there is something to this view, though prophecy also draws upon urban experience and argument. If the prophet sometimes looks at the city from a distance, he more often looks only at the city's rich and powerful citizens from a distance, that is, from the perspective of the men and women they oppressed. He then invokes values that even the oppressors pretend to share. Amos's main charge, his critical message, is not that the rich live well but that they live well at the expense of the poor. They have forgotten not only the laws of the covenant but the bond itself, the principle of solidarity: "They are not grieved for the hurt of Joseph" (6:6). More than this: they are themselves responsible for the hurt of Joseph; they are guilty of the Egyptian crime of oppression.

Amos's word for "oppress" is *'ashok;* he uses the Exodus word *lahatz* only once (6:14), when he is describing what will happen to Israel at the hands of an unnamed foreign power. The shift in terminology suggests nicely how Amos (or unknown speakers or writers before him) responds, within the tradition, to a new social experience. *Lahatz* means "to press down, to squeeze, to crush, to constrain, to coerce." The range of meanings evoked by

19. See, e.g., Blenkensopp, *History of Prophecy*, p. 95; Henry McKeating, *The Cambridge Bible Commentary: Amos, Hosea, Micah* (Cambridge: Cambridge University Press, 1971), p. 5.

'ashok is quite different: "to maltreat, to exploit, to wrong, to injure, to extort, to defraud." *Lahatz* has political connotations; '*ashok* has economic ones. Of course, Egyptian oppression was also economic in character, and in eighth century Israel and Judah the oppression of the poor was upheld by the monarchic regimes. Amos condemns both the "great houses" and the "palaces." But the primary experience was of tyranny in Egypt, of extortion and exploitation in Amos's own time. The new bondage had its origin in commerce—usury, indebtedness, default, and confiscation; its setting was more significantly the market than the state. Amos addresses himself specifically to avaricious merchants:

> Hear this, O ye that would swallow the needy
> And destroy the poor of the land,
> Saying, When will the new moon be gone, that we
>   may sell grain?
> And the Sabbath, that we may set forth corn,
> Making the ephah small and the shekel great,
> And falsifying the balances of deceit?
> That we may buy the poor for silver,
> And the needy for a pair of shoes,
> And sell the refuse of the corn.   *(8:4–6)*

The address, is doubly specific: to avaricious *Israelite* merchants, who can hardly wait for the end of Israel's holy days, when business dealings were forbidden, so that they can return to the business of extortion and fraud. Amos suggests hard questions. What kind of religion is it that provides only temporary and intermittent restraints on avarice and oppression? What is the quality of worship if it does not direct the heart toward goodness? As the prophet describes them, the oppressors of the poor and needy are scrupulously "orthodox." They observe the festival of the new moon, they keep the Sabbath, they attend the religious assemblies, offer the required sacrifices, join in the hymns that accompany the priestly rites. But all this is mere hypocrisy if it does not translate into everyday conduct in accordance with the covenantal code. Ritual observance alone is not what God requires of Israel. Pointing toward the real requirement, Amos evokes the memory of the Exodus: "Did ye bring unto Me sacrifices and offerings in the wilderness forty years, O house of Israel?" (5:25). In the Exodus story as we have it, they did; perhaps Amos had access to an alternative tradition.[20] But the practice of sacrifice is not, in any case, what was to be learned from the experience of liberation. Indeed, if oppression continues, nothing has been learned, however many animals are sacrificed.

This is the standard form of social criticism, and though later critics rarely achieve the angry poetry of the prophets, we can recognize in their work the same intellectual structure: the identification of public pronouncements and respectable opinion as hypocritical, the attack upon actual behavior and institutional arrangements, the search for core values (to which hypocrisy is always a clue), the demand for an everyday life in accordance with the core. The critic begins with revulsion and ends with affirmation:

> I hate, I despise your feasts,
> And I will take no delight in your solemn assemblies.
> Yea, though ye offer me burnt-offerings and your
> meal-offerings,
> I will not accept them . . .
> Take thou away from me the noise of thy songs;
> And let me not hear the melody of thy psalteries.
> But let justice well up as waters,
> And righteousness as a mighty stream.   *(5:21–24)*

20. McKeating, *Amos, Hosea, Micah*, p. 47.

The only purpose of the ceremonies is to remind the people of their moral commitments: God's law and the wilderness covenant. If that purpose is not served, then the ceremonies are of no use. Less than no use: for they generate among rich and avaricious Israelites a false sense of security—as if they were safe from divine wrath. The prophecies of doom, which make up so much of Amos's message, are designed to dispel that sense, to shatter the confidence of the conventionally pious: "Woe to them that are at ease in Zion" (6:1). Neither "woe" nor "hate" constitutes the substance of Amos's argument, however; the substance is "justice" and "righteousness."

But how does the prophet know that justice and righteousness are the core values of the Israelite tradition? Why not pilgrimage and sacrifice, song and solemnity? Why not ritual decorum and deference to God's priests? Presumably if Amaziah had offered a positive defense of his own activities at Beth-El, he would have given us a different picture of Israelite values. How then would the argument between Amaziah and Amos move toward closure? Both priest and prophet could cite texts—there is never a lack of texts— and both would find supporters in the crowd that gathered at the shrine. I have argued that disagreements of this sort do not in fact move toward closure, not at least definitive closure. Nor would they even if God himself were to intervene, for all he can provide is another text, subject to interpretation exactly like the earlier ones: "It is not in heaven." Still, we can recognize good and bad arguments, strong and weak interpretations, along the way. In this case it is significant that Amaziah makes no positive claims at all. His silence is a kind of admission that Amos has provided a convincing account of Israelite religion—also perhaps that he has found, as Greenberg says, advocates in

the hearts of the people. That does not end the disagreement, and not only because the prophet is apparently
forced to leave Beth-El, while Amaziah continues his
priestly routines. The claim that God is better served by
scrupulous worship of himself than by just dealings with
one's fellows, even if it is only made implicitly, has an
enduring appeal: worship is easier than justice. But Amos
has won a kind of victory, the only kind that is available:
he has evoked the core values of his audience in a powerful
and plausible way. He suggests an identification of the
poor in Israel with the Israelite slaves in Egypt and so
makes justice the primary religious demand. Why else did
God deliver the people, *this people,* from the house of
bondage?

AMOS'S PROPHECY is social criticism because it challenges
the leaders, the conventions, the ritual practices of a particular society and because it does so in the name of values
recognized and shared in that same society.[21] I have already distinguished this sort of prophecy from the sort
represented by Jonah in Nineveh: Jonah is a mere messenger who makes no appeal to social values, though he may
appeal, without saying so, to a minimal code, a kind of
international law. He is not a missionary, carrying with
him an alternative doctrine; he does not try to convert the
people of Nineveh to Israel's religion, to bring them into

21. Cf. Raymond Geuss's preferred version (not the only version) of critical
theory: "A critical theory is addressed to members of *this* particular social group
. . . it describes *their* epistemic principles and *their* ideal of the 'good life' and
demonstrates that some belief they hold is reflectively unacceptable for agents
who hold their epistemic principles and a source of frustration for agents who are
trying to realize this particular kind of 'good life.'" *Idea of a Critical Theory,*
p. 63.

the Sinai covenant. He just represents the minimal code (and God, its minimal author, who can have for the Ninevans none of the historical specificity that he has for the Israelites). We can think of Jonah as a minimalist critic; we do not really know what sorts of changes he required in the life of Nineveh, but they were presumably nowhere near so extensive as those required by Amos in Israel.

What makes the difference is Amos's membership. His criticism goes deeper than Jonah's because he knows the fundamental values of the men and women he criticizes (or because he tells them a plausible story about which of their values ought to be fundamental). And since he in turn is recognized as one of them, he can call them back to their "true" path. He suggests reforms that they can undertake while still remaining fellow members of the same society. Amos can, of course, be read differently: the prophecies of doom are so powerful and unrelenting that, on some interpretations, they overwhelm any possible argument for repentance and reform. And then the pleas for justice and the promises of divine comfort at the end seem unconvincing—as if they come (as many commentators believe, at least of the promises) from another hand.[22] The animating passion of the book as a whole, however, is surely a deep concern for "the hurt of Joseph," a powerful sense of solidarity, a commitment to the covenant that makes Israel Israel. Amos is a critic not only because of his anger but also because of his concern. He aims at an internal reformation that will bring the new oppression of Israel, or of poor and needy Israelites, to an end. That is the social meaning he has in mind when he repeats (or anticipates)

22. May, *Amos*, pp. 164–165. Cf. McKeating, *Amos, Hosea, Micah*, pp. 69–70.

the Deuteronomic injunction, "Seek good, and not evil, that ye may live" (5:15; cf. Deut. 30:15–20).

Amos also prophesies against nations other than Israel. Here he is a critic from the outside, like Jonah, and he limits himself to external behavior, violations of some sort of international law. I do not mean to suggest, however, that the provisions of Israel's covenant have no general validity. One could no doubt abstract universal rules from them—above all, one universal rule: *do not oppress the poor* (for oppression is, as Weber writes, "the pre-eminent vice" in the eyes of the Israelite prophets).[23] And then one could judge and condemn the oppression of Syrians, or Philistines, or Moabites, by their avaricious fellows in the same way that the prophets judge and condemn the oppression of Israelites. But not, in fact, in the same way—not with the same words, images, references; not with regard to the same practices and religious principles. For the power of a prophet like Amos derives from his ability to say what oppression means, how it is experienced, in this time and place, and to explain how it is connected with other features of a shared social life. One of his most important arguments, for example, is about oppression and religious observance: it is entirely possible to trample upon the poor and to observe the Sabbath. From this he concludes that the laws against oppression take precedence over the Sabbath laws. The hierarchy is specific; it invites the prophet's listeners to remember that the Sabbath was instituted so "that thy manservant and thy maidservant may rest as well as thou" (Deut. 5:14). Prophecy would have little life, and little effect, if it could not evoke memories of this sort. We might think of prophecy, then,

23. *Ancient Judaism*, p. 281.

as an academic exercise. In a strange country, Amos would resemble Samson in Gaza. Not eyeless, but tongueless: he might indeed see the oppression, but he would not be able to give it a name or speak about it to the hearts of the people.

Other nations, of course, can read and admire the Israel-ite prophets, translate the prophecies into their own lan-guage (footnoting the references), and find analogies in their own society for the practices the prophets condemn. Just how wide the actual range of reading and admiration is, I am not sure. It obviously does not coincide with the possible range, and it may well be limited to those nations whose history is in some significant sense continuous with the history of Israel. In principle, though, it could extend further than that. What would it mean if it did? It is un-likely that distant readers would learn from the prophets a set of abstract rules, or again a single rule: don't oppress the poor. If they knew what oppression was (if they could translate the Hebrew word *'ashok*), they would already know that much. The rule, though it might have different references and applications, would be familiar. More likely, distant readers would be moved to imitate the prac-tice of prophecy (or perhaps to listen in a new way to their own prophets). It is the practice, not the message, that would be repeated. Readers might learn to be social critics; the criticism, however, would be their own. Indeed, the message would have to be different if the practice was to be the same—else it would lack the historical reference and moral specificity that prophecy (and social criticism) re-quires.

The case is different with regard to Amos's prophecies against the nations. Here it is precisely the message, the minimal code, that gets repeated: do not violate treaties, do not kill innocent women and children, do not transport whole nations into involuntary exile. Confirmed from many sides, these rules are incorporated into a law of nations that is not much more extensive than the "international" law of Amos's time. But their prophetic utterance is quickly forgotten. For the utterance is a mere assertion and not an interpretation or elaboration of the law; reference and specificity, though Amos provides a brief version of both, are in fact unnecessary. Can a useful distinction be drawn between these two sorts of rules, those against violence and those against oppression? The two have the same linguistic form. Each of them extends toward the other, and there will always be considerable overlap between them. The minimal code is relevant to and presumably plays a part in the development of more substantive social values; and the code itself takes on a particular form depending on how those values develop. Yet the two are not the same. The rules against violence arise from the experience of international as well as internal relations; the rules against oppression arise from internal relations alone. The first rules regulate our contacts with all humanity, strangers as well as citizens; the second regulate only our common life. The first are stereotyped in form and application; they are set against a background of standard expectations, based on a narrow range of standard experiences (among which war is the most prominent). The second are complex in form and various in application; they are set against a background of multiple and conflicting expectations, rooted in a long and dense social history. The first rules tend toward universality, the second toward particularity.

It is a mistake, then, to praise the prophets for their universalist message. For what is most admirable about them is their particularist quarrel, which is also, they tell us, God's quarrel, with the children of Israel. Here they invested their anger and their poetic genius. The line that Amos attributes to God, "You only have I known of all the families of the earth," could have come from his own heart. He knows one nation, one history, and it is that knowledge which makes his criticism so rich, so radical, so concrete. We can, again, abstract the rules and apply them to other nations, but that is not the "use" that Amos invites. What he invites is not application but reiteration. Each nation can have its own prophecy, just as it has its own history, its own deliverance, its own quarrel with God:

> Have I not brought up Israel out of the land of Egypt,
> And the Philistines from Caphtor,
> And Aram from Kir?   *(9:7)*

INDEX OF NAMES